Praise for *Don*

T0288503

"Dr. Mary Ann Smialek has pr[o]
sive resource to help their childr[e]......... .... *Miss*
the Bus! is filled with practical, realistic advice that addresses
such important topics as motivation, discipline, homework,
home–school partnerships, self-esteem, and self-respect. I am
certain that parents as well as teachers will return to this book
over and over again for the invaluable information it contains."

— **Robert Brooks,** Ph. D., faculty at
Harvard Medical School, author of
The Self-Esteem Teacher, and coauthor
of *Raising Resilient Children*

"*Don't Miss the Bus!* supplies useful and practical strategies that
parents can use as they lay the foundation of a child's school
success. Dr. Smialek sets the stage nicely for the importance of
the home–school connection and gives valuable suggestions
for how parents and teachers can work together in the best
interest of children."

— **Robert J. Wittman,** executive director
of community education,
Robbinsdale Area Schools

"*Don't Miss the Bus!* shares with parents an easy-to-read, user
friendly resource on what they can do to support their children's educational development. Importantly, Dr. Smialek
focuses on what parents can do both *at home and at school* to
support children's learning. *Don't Miss the Bus!* emphasizes the
important role that parents play in ensuring a quality educational experience for their children."

— **Karen L. Mapp,** Ed. D., president,
Institute for Responsive Education

"*Don't Miss the Bus!* is thoughtful and supportive in its approach; practical, direct, and clear in its action plans. Dr. Smialek shares strategies for school success that are easy to read, understand, and follow. This guide will help steer parents and educators to positive home-school partnerships that can lead to the development of comprehensive community schools."

— **Martin J. Blank,** staff director,
Coalition for Community Schools
Institute for Educational Leadership

"In its review of current research, the National Center for Family and Community Connections with Schools has found that students with involved parents—no matter what their income or background—tend to do better in school, stay in school longer, and like school more. In *Don't Miss the Bus!* parents will find a myriad of practical ideas and suggested activities from a seasoned educator to help them become meaningfully involved in their children's education. Dr. Smialek includes ideas and actions that can help parents build trusting relationships with their children and school personnel that will lead to increased student success in school and life."

— **Catherine Jordan,** program manager,
Southwest Educational Development
Laboratory

Don't Miss the Bus!

Don't Miss the Bus!

Steering Your Child
to Success in School

MARY ANN SMIALEK

TAYLOR TRADE PUBLISHING
A ScarecrowEducation Book
Lanham • New York • Oxford

Published by Taylor Trade Publishing
A Member of the Rowman & Littlefield Publishing Group
4501 Forbes Boulevard, Suite 200
Lanham, Maryland 20706

Distributed by National Book Network

Library of Congress Cataloging-in-Publication Data

Smialek, Mary Ann, 1946–
    Don't miss the bus! : steering your child to success in school /
Mary Ann Smialek.
        p. cm.
    "A co-publication by Taylor Trade Publishing and ScarecrowEducation."
    Includes bibliographical references.
    ISBN: 978-1-58979-053-7
    1. Education—Parent participation. 2. Academic achievement. I. Title.
    LB1048.5.S64 2003
    371.19'2—dc21   2002156347

♾™ The paper used in this publication meets the minimum requirements of American National Standard for Information Sciences—Permanence of Paper for Printed Library Materials, ANSI/NISO Z39.48–1992.
Manufactured in the United States of America.

Interior design by Andrea Reider
Chapter illustrations by Andrew Brozyna

To my family—my husband Bob, for his support, guidance, and assistance with the creation of the book title and for his collaboration on the chapter titles, and my son Rob, for his technical support and encouragement—and to all the parents I had the pleasure of working with over the years.

CONTENTS

FOREWORD

Preparing children to grow up and become happy, successful, functional adults has become increasingly difficult for parents. For example, children today attend school as many hours per week as their grandparents. The process of education has become increasingly more complex and demanding. From a very young age, children are bombarded with information from sources that extend far beyond the family and school. The advertising industry spends $12 billion a year marketing directly to children. Children see advertisements nearly everywhere, from the print media to television and the Internet, and even in their classrooms. Legislation on state and federal levels has mandated schools must appropriately educate all children. Current statistics suggest that more children than ever before are struggling academically, emotionally, and behaviorally in school. In turn, schools are recognizing that the foundation for successful students lies beyond the classroom, in the critical foundation parents provide for their children.

Increasingly, parents are seeking resources to understand the educational system, to interact in a positive way with teachers, and, most importantly, to help their children develop a resilient mind-set and experience school success. Dr. Mary Ann Smialek has responded to this need in *Don't Miss the Bus!: Steering Your Child to Success in School*. Dr. Smialek writes from experience as a parent and professional. She understands the inner workings of the educational system and the stress and demands placed on parents and families today. Focused on assisting parents help all children, this book is eminently practical, reasoned, and reasonable. It will be of equal help to parents of children performing well as to those who struggle in school with learning, emotional, or behavioral problems. The book begins by helping parents understand the aspects of their role in helping their children be successful in school. Dr. Smialek outlines a reasoned set of parental expectations and responsibilities. She offers a series of steps to help parents prepare their children for school success. She provides strategies and tips to enhance motivation and interest in school, completion of homework, and success in the classroom. She provides a set of guideposts for parents to strengthen home-school partnerships. Beyond the classroom, she offers parents a set of strategies to discipline effectively and, most importantly, to help each child build a true sense of self-esteem. Increasingly, educators, mental health professionals, and researchers are demonstrating that children's mind-set toward school and their attitudes and beliefs about their capabilities, teachers, and the work placed in front of them represents the key ingredient in school success.

Finally, this is the first book to offer a set of guidelines for parents to understand and set appropriate limits for their children's use and interaction with the Internet. This section alone makes this a valuable book. *Don't Miss the Bus!* is a book that I will enthusiastically endorse and recommend to the families with which I work. It offers a valuable road map to help parents prepare and guide their children to a successful school career.

Sam Goldstein, Ph.D.
Clinical Assistant Professor
University of Utah

INTRODUCTION

Would you like to change your relationship with your children to a more positive one? Would you like to reduce stress and create more balance in your life and the lives of your children? What would your life be like if you had the know-how and the confidence to change your outlook and "method of operation" with your children? Would you like happy, confident, and successful children in school?

If you answered "yes" to any one of these questions, then read on! More and more parents would like to avoid the roadblocks to their children's school success. Help is just down the road at the Bus Stops along the way! Whether you are a father working sixty hours a week, an overworked single mother trying to raise a family by yourself, or a parent who is just plain tired of feeling stressed out and pressed for time, *Don't Miss the Bus!* is for you. It will guide you in your choices about how to achieve and enjoy quality parent-child relationships. The strategies in this book are geared for parents of children who are in elementary and middle school. You have the power to help your children be happy and successful at home and school. The secret to that success is just around the corner!

What do you do and where do you turn when you decide to improve your parent-child relationship? Overcoming the obstacles to your children's school success is the focus of this book. It contains the "how-to" and the action plans to support you on your journey. If you are willing to work hard and invest the necessary time and energy in this process, I promise you that your life and the lives of your children will change dramatically. You can make the shift, put yourself in the driver's seat, and take charge of how you guide your children to school success. You can enjoy a life with a positive, parent-child relationship and I'd like to show you how. Stay focused on our journey with the ideas and strategies in this book that will get you from where you are now to where you want to be. With the right purpose, knowledge, and tools, you can make even the most challenging situations work for you and your children. If you are serious about improving the quality of your relations with your children and guiding them to success in school, this book provides an important element for your success: the guiding hand of a teacher who helped other parents on their journey.

School Is a Team Effort

The teacher's job is to teach.

The child's job is to learn.

The parent's job is to help the child

be ready and able to learn.

It's Time to Wake up and Get Ready!

Parent Expectations and Responsibilities

○ What are my expectations for my children at home and at school?

○ What are my responsibilities as a parent?

1

A S A PARENT, you have the most important job in this world: to love, nurture, and guide your children. While it is an awesome role, many times it is not a joyous one. It is filled with self-doubt, mixed messages, and often just a plain lack of knowledge.

Yes, you want the best of everything for your children, including success at school. You are doing the best you can in your particular situation, but sometimes it is just not working. Your life has numerous demands—too many to enumerate. The list of things to do goes on and on, and you secretly say to yourself, "Am I doing my best for my children?" "How do I know if I'm on the right track?" "Am I doing what's best?" "Am I doing my part in the home-school connection?"

Whether you believe it or not, you have the power to orchestrate your children's school success story. Yes! All the comprehensive curriculum, award-winning teachers, Blue Ribbon Schools, and the use of e-learning programs can't turn around the personal challenges you face every-day to ensure your young ones' school success. The challenges that you face are important to you and crucial to your children. If you don't do something positive to reach your children and what affects their journey to school success, no one else will. The buck stops here—with you!

Make no mistake about it, what is done in schools can never replace the education that you give your children. *You* are your child's first and best teacher. Schools will only augment the sound educational foundation that you have laid down. What occurs in the years before your children go to school has a decisive effect on what happens in the following school years. As a parent, you must learn to accept the responsibility of educating your children from the time they enter this world.

Your children's school situation really can be different. You, as a parent, have the pivotal advantage to make this happen. Up until now, you just haven't had the focus, the knowledge, and the strategies to make things better. If what you're doing now isn't working, you owe it to your children and to yourself to consider an alternative approach. Ask yourself these questions: "Am I going from day to day just reacting to what's going on in my life?" "Have I settled for what is easy and safe for the time being?" "Am I just managing challenges with my children as they come along?" If you answered "yes," there is a solution to your indecisiveness and ineffectiveness. You need a plan for changing your children's school problems into rewarding emotional, social, and academic successes.

This book is designed to furnish you with a map you need for the direction that you seek. Remember, you are accountable for your children's smooth ride throughout the school journey, whether or not you want to believe it! It's not too late. There is still time to get organized so that you and your children are not left at the bus stop, out in the cold, alone! Keep in mind, the bigger the challenges you and your children are experiencing now, the bigger their downslide if they are ignored or mismanaged.

Time for a reality check! The world has changed! It's a much different world from the one that your parents and grandparents knew. Today, we are all "caught up" in a fast-paced, ever-changing society and our children's needs are often lost in the shuffle. You are sometimes forced to put a Band-Aid on your young ones' school problems and neglect the basics underlying a desired home environment that is conducive to facilitate well-rounded and happy children. When it comes to managing your own life and helping your young ones learn how to manage theirs, you are "out of sync" and you still keep pretending that you can handle things. When you finally give up that notion and realize that you need some clear, practical, and proven approaches to deal with your children, things will start to turn around.

Why should you pay attention to what I have to share? First, I am a parent. Second, I am a teacher. I have taught in both regular and special education classes for many years. I have seen firsthand how parenting has changed over the years. Nonetheless, good, basic parenting skills don't change by outside forces of our society. Good parenting is often tried and tested and sometimes does come up short of expectations. We all fall victim to the disappointments of life from time to time.

What is important to remember is that you ultimately have in your power the will and the motivation to secure a better home-school life for your children. The strategies in this book will show you how. If what you are doing now is not working, be willing to move your position and "shift gears" in favor of a fresh, new direction. Follow the suggestions at each Bus Stop. You can always go back to your old way of doing things, but know that it's worth a try to change your child-management methods for the better. You may be delightfully surprised with the results of doing so.

The time for your children's school success has come! No matter if your children have a diagnosed learning or attention problem, you've got what it takes to turn the situation around. You have everything in you to make this change in your children's life. Your children are worth the time that you will take and the effort you will make from now on. You will be in control of the situation once you figure out that there is a definite formula for school success. How can you gain this control? Acquire the knowledge that you need to create the results you desire.

First, you must determine what is expected of your children in school to be successful and what you must facilitate to make this happen. You must be willing to learn things you don't know, so that you can begin to make better choices and decisions for your children. No matter how much you think you are in control, if you haven't acquired the certain skills to work successfully with your children, your trek will be futile and you will "miss the bus"! Sometimes, the most difficult part in learning something new is unlearning something old. Acknowledge and accept accountability for your role in creating success for your children at school. Learn how to make and implement better decisions so that you and your children will have more rewarding experiences and a happier future.

What can a parent or other concerned adults do to guide children to school success, especially those who don't have strong financial means or a reliable family support system? Amazingly, most of the strategies that help your children the most do not require money. Parental efforts including care, attention, time, patience, and most of all love, are all free and within your reach.

The road signs at the end of each Bus Stop offer tips and techniques that cost nothing, but they will make all the difference in the world to your children. Most parents do guide their children instinctively, while some have to learn methods that are effective. Some ideas seem too small or insignificant to many parents to be worth the trouble to follow. Keep in mind that they are all essential to your youngsters' development. School success depends greatly on how well your children have learned the prerequisite skills needed for academic readiness and development.

From the very beginning, children should be taught values in unequivocal terms. They want to know that there are limits—moral as well as physical—to the world in which they live. They should be told not to touch a hot oven and that it is wrong to play in the street. They should also be instructed that it is wrong to lie, cheat, and steal. They should be taught not to bully others and to be tolerant of others who are different from them. It is sad to say that much of what is wrong in schools today can be attributed to weak or warped values that originated in the children's home environment. In teaching children standards of right and wrong, young people will more easily accept the discipline necessary to learn in school if they are taught these values in the home environment. Make no mistake about it, much of the failure in our schools is ethical rather than academic. Schools can never supply the quality, the values, and the amount of learning that must take place in the home long before children walk through the school doors for the first time.

In this new "Knowledge Age" era, schools are working under increased accountability, fewer resources, shrinking budgets, larger class sizes, and a limited support staff. Simply put, school districts are operating under greater scrutiny than ever before. The expectation is that schools must "do better" if their graduates are to compete in the real world of the Information Age. Consequently, at no time in the history of American education has the need been so important for you, as a parent, to do your part—your job—to love, guide, and nurture your children. This is the basis for not only successful children and families, but also for the development of the necessary home-school partnerships for children's school success and lifetime achievement. To do so will ensure that your children will not "miss the bus"!

It's not too late. You still have time to hop on the bus for your destination: your children's school success. First of all, you need to know the rules of the road, avoid road-blocks and detours, and have a good map to safely get you there.

You love your children and know very well your responsibility to provide for them. In the past, parents understood something that perplexes many of today's parents: they were not only obliged to feed and shelter their young ones, but also to teach them self-control, ethics, and a meaningful way of understanding the world.

What has happened to the lost art of parenting? Why is it that so many parents have turned themselves into their children's friends? Try to avoid the thoughts: "I don't want to upset my children by telling them 'no,'" or "I feel so guilty when I discipline them." Don't slip past the recognition of your children's secret longing for a structure that they can believe in and live by. It's time to drive out your own fear and accept your responsibility to teach your young ones self-respect and self-control. To pass these values on to your children, you must be sure that these values are important enough for you to pursue with conviction. You must firmly define a moral universe for your children and communicate the "rules of the road."

In the end, it is your children who will pay the price for your refusal to seriously engage in your parenting rights and responsibilities. It is an enormous price! When you shirk your parenting duties, you are not only depriving the clarity and sound judgment that your children crave, but you are also denying them of their right to a childhood and all that it stands for.

Today, more than ever, an increasing number of children are not succeeding in school as well as in life. Far too many of them are discouraged, do not accept responsibility, have low self-esteem, and lack motivation for learning. These behaviors most always become a source of frustration, failure, and fatigue for both youngsters and parents. Many of these problems that families experience are either organizational or a result of just plain lack of know-how, rather than academic in nature.

There is good news! *Don't Miss the Bus!* can help you make a difference in your life and in the lives of your children. You can make an impact in your children's personal and school success, a success that will continue throughout life's ups and downs. The strategies in this book are methods that I have observed and practiced for many years and have found practical, workable, and successful with both students and parents. I will share with you what really does work: ideas, techniques, and even some anecdotes that can assist you in improving your children's behavior, responsibility, and academic achievement. You will find caring, experience, and wisdom at each Bus Stop.

This book will serve as a road map to guide you in meeting the challenges of parenting during the school years. Applying the practical ideas and using the tips and methods presented in this book, you will have a doable plan that will give you the skills and confidence you need to help your children grow into being self-confident, well-adjusted, and successful individuals. You will learn how to make good choices for yourself as a parent and will be able to communicate these choices to your children. Most importantly, you will secure two valuable tools to help sustain you on your journey: knowledge and action. This book also provides clear, practical, and achievable strategies specific to making you a loving, consistent, and effective guardian of your children's best interest.

The strategies presented in this book for successful parenting to facilitate your children's school success are in no way exhaustive, but they have been tested and found to be valid. They have been proven to establish a mind-set and a direction to bring about the outcomes that you want for your children. Throughout the pages of the book, I will focus on what you need to know: the skills to establish the right environment for your children to be confident, caring, and *ready* to "get on the bus" and learn at school.

Now, it's time to get ready! Be on time! and *Don't Miss the Bus!* All aboard for your destination. Your children need you to be an understanding, knowledgeable, and patient role model. Children learn best by example. Let's get ready for Bus Stop #2! Are you getting on the bus?

Don't Miss the Bus! in formulating expectations for your children and realizing what your responsibilities are as a parent!

Stop! Look! Take Action!

Accept Your Responsibility As a Parent

1. Do your part—your job: love, guide, and nurture your children.

2. Acknowledge and accept accountability for your role in your children's success.

3. Teach standards of right and wrong and values in unequivocal terms.
   - Teach by your good example
   - Be an understanding, knowledgeable, and patient role model
   - Teach, don't preach

Children have more need of models than critics.
—JOSEPH JOUBERT

Walk, Don't Run!

Four Steps to Good Parenting for School Success

○ How can I help my children be successful in school?

○ What are the Four Steps to Good Parenting for School Success?

○ What do I need to learn to make better decisions for my children?

2

START WITH A POSITIVE ATTITUDE

Focus on the benefits that your love, knowledge, and effort will help lessen conflict and tension in your home. Learn to trust yourself. This is an integral part of building a strong foundation that will allow you to guide your children on the road to school success. You must act in ways that make it clear for you that you have the power to guide your own choices and, consequently, the choices that your children will make. As you gain experience, you will become less attached to the opinions of both experts and nonexperts and more able to make the decisions that support what you ultimately want for your children: healthy, happy, and successful lives. Even if your actions are in the best interests of your children, fear can stop you in your tracks. We all have imaginations fueled by negativity. Decide to see your new attitude as one that gives values and something great to your children. When resistance or fear arises, refer to the strategies at each Bus Stop, and try again.

As you gain confidence in and are more comfortable with your "new view" of a positive home environment, take the next step. One of the most significant contributions you can make to the world is to empower your children to lead responsible lives. You can do this by modeling and offering guidance that will build your young ones' confidence and self-esteem. Increase your own awareness of the "rules" you reinforce. Cheryl Richardson, in her book *Stand up for Your Life,* gives good and sound advice when she points out that instead of you, as a child, being trained to follow rules that may have crushed your spirit, imagine what your life would have been like if you had been taught these instead:

- Be informed
- Stick with it
- Stop apologizing when you've done nothing wrong
- Be courageous
- Think big
- Be ambitious
- Be enthusiastic
- Be proud of yourself
- Keep your expectations high
- Go for it!

She states that her life would have been different had she been raised with these types of rules. She notes that she would have spoken up in school when she knew the answer to a teacher's question instead of feeling too insecure to raise her hand. She also mentioned that she would have performed in the high school plays that captured her imagination rather than relegating herself to the audience and longing to be on stage.

How would your life have been different? Give your children the opportunity to omit the "could have been" and the "should have been" thoughts from their minds. Give them a new set of rules by which to live.

You will have many opportunities during the day to encourage and implement these new rules. Discuss them with your children. Monitor and adjust them for maximum output. Integrate them into your daily routine. Watch what happens!

Another good way to foster a positive attitude is to acknowledge your children's strengths. Don't dwell on the negative issues. One of my graduate school professors often reminded the class: "Teach to the student's strengths. The weaknesses will take care of themselves." For an example of how this plays out in the real world, consider RJ, a student of mine. His handwriting was so illegible that on many occasions I couldn't read what he wrote. He was a most creative writer with much insight for whatever subject he was writing about, but others could not appreciate his work because they couldn't decipher his penmanship. Many times, I would have to have him read the story to me. I would compliment him on the flow of the paragraphs and the detail of events, and I especially commented on the humor he injected into some dull subject matter. Over the course of the year, he took such great pride in being a good writer and excellent speller that slowly, with my assistance, he practiced his penmanship skills on his own and with parental guidance. By the end of the year, he was one of the most legible handwriters in my class. Remember to point out your children's unique qualities regularly. There is an added bonus to this philosophy. By doing this, you teach young people to acknowledge both their own strengths and those of others.

Talk to your children and discuss that their failures and mistakes are "stepping-stones" to success. Encourage them to role-play with you as to how the situation in question could have had a better outcome. If you are "really brave," switch roles with your children when play-acting or role-playing. Permit your youngsters to be you and you take their role. This is an eye-opening experience to say the least. How quickly you'll see the results that you seek. It will give you valuable insight and just the information that you need to turn a negative situation around to a positive one and make your life and the lives of your children a little easier. You will gain a new understanding to guide them in the right direction toward success at home and in school.

Above all, stress the importance of family. It is important that small children feel secure with the encompassing love of your family. Share with your young ones that "family values" are the means by which society survives and communicates its moral and ethical lessons to the next generation. Teach your young ones to honor and cherish their own families as well as respect for the families of others. Family loyalty helps to build a strong sense of their own values and make them more secure when they're out in the world. Children who know who they are and what they're about will be more competent individuals and students.

CREATE A BALANCE IN YOUR LIFE

Most of the time, as a parent, you work on "overload." Take time for yourself! Take the time necessary for the "art of parenting." No, you are not being selfish! Use the same advice the flight attendants give their passengers when on board a departing flight. "Secure your own oxygen mask first, and then attend to your child." If things are not "right" with you first, they won't be "right" for your children in things that really matter. It is extremely important to manage your time wisely and ask for help when necessary. You can't possibly do everything yourself. Prioritize what needs to be done. Do what's most important first. If you run out of time, you'll get to those other things of lesser importance at another time when you're not experiencing a time crunch in your busy schedule.

Effective and efficient parenting takes time, sustained interest, and effort. At the same time that parents' working hours are increasing, emotional problems are on the increase among children. We live in an age of blurred boundaries and vanished time. The "art of parenting" suffers in this type of existence. We need to learn to get this important balance of time in proper perspective by doing the following actions:

- Turn off the cell phone. If the call is that important, the caller will call back.
- Turn off the computer, television, and video games. Play with your children. Use toys and games that require parent-child interaction.
- Set certain time periods when you can have one-on-one time with each of your children.

By going through these motions, you will be consciously willing yourself to slow down by talking to and most importantly listening to your children. In his book *The Superman Syndrome*, Robert Kam says that "parenting calls us to live at depth but we cannot live at depth when we live at speed." With a little creativity and a few fun activities, you can help put some passion into your kids' home and school performance and into their lives. Your children will realize that *you* really do care and that you really are interested in *them*.

A good start is to encourage children to pursue the things and subjects in which *they* are interested. That means supporting your children's development of hobbies and passions: playing with Lego blocks, baseball card collecting, participating in Boy or Girl Scouts, skateboarding—whatever your children enjoy.

When my nephew Ken (same age as my son) was reading chapter books late into the night at age seven, it was difficult to get my son Rob to read his reading assignment from school. At that time, his love was baseball card collecting. We went to card shows, card shops, and flea markets. My husband traveled a good deal for his job and was always on the lookout for that certain card that Rob needed to complete a set. During this period, to my dismay, I wasn't quite sure how well Rob could read so I got involved with him in a discussion about the cards. I progressed to reading the statistics on the cards to him, then, gradually he read them to me— on his own. Eventually, he graduated to reading baseball magazines and books that had more difficult words than were in his reading book at school. Using this strategy of encouraging reading through a child's interest paid off. It worked in my son's case!

Once you tap into your children's interests, you can weave in other things they should learn. There are a myriad of other ways to encourage and enhance educational experiences in your children's daily routine. Don't underestimate the importance of the family meal. Our hectic schedules don't always allow for this powerful exchange of ideas for affirmation, guidance, and discussion of alternative actions. The sharing of information at the dinner, lunch, or breakfast table brings the family closer, builds self-esteem, and the ever-important exchange of ideas. A significant lesson for your children to learn is to trust and honor their own feelings and actions. The payoff is the encouragement that is needed to talk about what goes on in their lives outside the family unit.

My son has always been an individual of a few words. One strategy that worked was to take him out for dinner to his favorite restaurant. I'm not quite sure if it was one thing more than another or a combination of things that made the real difference, but my son would actually talk to me about "things" without me asking him many questions to jump-start the conversation. This strategy worked every time for me. I still use it today and Rob is twenty-four years old.

Simplify your life and that of your children: create a balance. Another good idea is to write down all the activities in which you and your children are involved. With your children's input, rank these activities from the most beneficial and desired to the least important. Estimate how much time it would take for the top seven activities. Include practice time, preparation time, and travel time.

You must consider another important factor: the value of each activity. Tutoring and enrichment classes improve self-esteem. Sports can improve your children's physical self-concept and team-building skills and can encourage good health practices. Music and art lessons stimulate an interest in the appreciation of the arts, creativity, confidence, and high self-esteem. Take time from your busy schedule to plan a balanced one for you and your children. If you do so, you will secure a plan that will not frustrate you or them and will definitely help prepare your children today for tomorrow's success in a more resourceful, calm, and timely manner.

Help your children develop ongoing relationships. Create regular daily, weekly, or monthly rituals that bring you together as a family, whatever your family unit is. The stereotypical family—mom, dad, two children (one girl and one boy), a dog, and, of course, the station wagon— is not the only viable family unit that exists today. The families of today take on many different forms and variations.

Everyday experiences can also be learning lessons. If you're going to a Chinese restaurant, look up China and its regions on the Internet together. Shopping is another great learning experience (in addition to being therapy for you). Money is a great teaching tool.

When shopping for a winter coat for my son when he was six years old, he saw a parka that he liked. He followed my example from previous shopping excursions: He first touched the fabric, looked at the price tag, and said, "This will be warm but there are too many numbers on the tag." I'm not sure if the price really mattered to him then, but he had learned another shopping lesson from me over the years, one that was more important in the bigger scheme of things. When evaluating something he wanted, following my example, he'd ask himself: "Do I really need this?" I always made the distinction between wants and needs to him. I guess he was listening! Clearly, everyday experiences can breathe life into occasions for school learning.

Opportunities abound everywhere to show your children the relevance of learning to live in general. This practical application of life skills will enhance out-of-school interests that will in turn increase the passion your children bring to related academic subjects. These personal, leisure-time interests and activities enrich school discussions and lessons. In many of my reading and math classes, my students shared their experiences about when they were at the mall, the beach, at camp, helping dad, doing chores, and so on. They always added much enrichment to the lesson in a way that I, as a teacher, could not have. Don't underestimate the power of enriching learning times that happen outside of school. They usually relate so well and add so much to a lesson. An added bonus is that your children's self-confidence and self-esteem is boosted beyond measure when they can contribute to a classroom discussion or project.

What do kids really want from their parents? Ask them; you will be surprised. According to Ellen Galinsky, in her book *Ask the Children*, most parents thought that their youngsters would say that they wanted more time with mom and/or dad. The fact is that only 10 percent of the children respondents indicated they wanted more time with mom and 15 percent said they wanted more time with dad. What most children wanted was that their parents were less stressed and tired when they did spend time with them. Only 2 percent of parents guessed that their children might respond in this way. Create a balance in your life. Take time for what's really important to you and what is best for your children. If you need some ideas, ask your children what is important to them! They will tell you!

REMEMBER: YOU ARE THE BOSS!

Do yourself and your children a favor. Establish firm, clear boundaries that leave no doubt you are in control. Your children need limits. Learn to say: "I love you, that's why I sometimes say 'no.'" First, know what you want from your children. Let your thoughts, words, and actions express this knowledge:

- Strengthen your relationship with your children by always telling the truth and standing by it.
- Use challenging situations to make you even more confident and stronger.
- Expect the best from your children. Don't give into their wants and desires. Focus on their needs, but do give them choices.
- Teach your children self-discipline and patience by encouraging them to stop and assess their circumstances before reacting to difficult situations. This will help them become aware of how their actions may affect others.
- Help your young ones to develop the courage to see the world through their own eyes instead of yours or the eyes of others.
- Help them to respect and understand their differences by example in modeling tolerant behaviors.

This is an example, sad but true, about how respect is reciprocal. Mrs. Kiefer called during my morning math class. The secretary asked if I could take the call because

Mrs. Kiefer was extremely upset and wanted to talk with me immediately. Thinking that there must be an emergency, I took the call. Mrs. Kiefer blurted out after I said "hello": "I'm so upset and hurt. At the bus stop, Paul called me a b——. I think he learned it from his older brother and his father. I don't know what to do, so I called you. I don't know where that little b—— gets off, calling me a b—— anyway!"

In this situation, you could use an "I message" to tell your children how you feel. It is quite effective to say: "When you call me names, I feel discouraged. It seems like you don't respect me." Another strong statement for this circumstance is: "I think you're really mad at me for some reason. Let's talk about it." Above all, children learn from your example. If you call them names, oftentimes your little ones will think that it's okay to call you names as well. Be cognizant of this fact and always be respectful of your children, if you want the same respect in return.

Keep in mind that in any good relationship—husband and wife, employer and employee, or parent and child—respect and trust is the basis of that relationship. When there is a foundation built on trust and respect, the relationship takes on added dimensions. It starts with: "You do this and that." Then moves to: "I will do it because I'm not sure you will do it." And progresses to: "Together, we can work it out."

When your children are disrespectful, try these strategies:

- Calm down before you respond. Give your children time to cool off, too.
- Start with: "It hurts me when you speak to me that way. I think we'd better talk things over. Let me know when you're ready to discuss things."
- Listen, really listen, to what they have to say. Keep the communication lines open and accessible. Be open to their ideas and, by all means, explain yours.
- Look for underlying causes for their behavior. Try to get to the root of the problem.
- Give them a hug to reassure them. Tell them that you want things to change, that you love them, but, in no uncertain terms, that you do not like their actions.
- Make a plan to avert this type of behavior in the future. Discuss alternatives—a very important step. Consider how "we" can problem solve together. Ask the question: "How do we keep from hurting one another?"
- Lay out some ground rules and consequences if these are broken.

When a disagreement arises, remember you are the boss but you can be flexible and listen to what your children have to say without interrupting. Remain rational and promote rationality in your youngsters. At all cost, avoid reacting defensively. In giving long explanations, you'll loose your young ones' attention. Don't make the mistake of trying to get your children to understand or convince them that you are being "fair." It is a waste of time! They are just not there—in that place—in their development to fully appreciate what you are trying to say and do. They can't even imagine that the actions you are taking are in their best interest. While following this strategy, you are shaping your own behavior with the payoffs you are getting in shaping your children's behavior. Find and control these payoffs, and you control the behavior, whether it is your behavior pattern or your children's. If—but only if—you understand and embrace this concept, your dealings with your children will dramatically improve over time. Next, set a course of action and don't give up when things don't go well the first time. Engage in a little self-talk: "There will be some setbacks, but I'll deal with them. I did not have immediate success, but I will stay on course. I am capable of making a difference in my children's life. Yes, I am, I am going to do it."

Put It Your Way and Firmly

Make no mistake about it, discipline is first and foremost a matter of effective communication. Give instructions to your children properly and be amazed at the results you get. Proper communication will prevent those undesired behaviors your children sometime exhibit. Here are some strategies that will help produce the behaviors you want:

1. When you give instructions, don't phrase them in questions: "Let's get ready for bed, okay?" A better way to express this is: "It's almost bedtime," or "It's bath time now."

2. Give instructions that are direct when dealing with young children or to those who have attention problems. Your directions should be no longer than two commands. An ideal approach is to say: "First, clean up your room. When you're done, let me know and I'll tell you what's next."

3. Be specific when you tell your children what you expect of them and when you expect it done. An example of unclear communication to your children is: "I want you to be good at your school's Open House tonight." Say it in a way that your young ones will know exactly what you expect: "I want you to stay with Mom and Dad tonight at school. You can play with your friends tomorrow." Another illustration of this strategy is: "Take out the trash sometime today, pickup is tomorrow." Your instruction will be more effective when you phrase it: "I want you to take out the trash when you come home from school today."

4. Don't express your instructions in form of wishes ("I wish you would stop . . ."), reasons, or explanations ("If you eat now, you can play later."). You're going to have to work on this one! It's a natural inclination to say more than what is needed in giving children directions. Remember, young ones need additional processing time even for two commands at a time. Also, it's more productive not to "overload" an older child with too many instructions at one time. I have found that giving "short and sweet" directions gets things done faster and more efficiently. Try to remember when you practice this strategy that practice makes

perfect! This technique of giving short and direct instructions to your children will really payoff in getting what you want done and will not frustrate either you or your youngsters. It is very powerful to phrase directions to your children that are specific and concise. Here are some examples:

- "It's time to say good-bye and go home."
- "Stop hitting the dog."
- "You need to pick up your toys and put them away."
- "Close your mouth when you chew gum."
- "Cut the grass after school today."

Resolve now that you will make the effort and be persistent in your goals in guiding your children to school success. It will happen, but not by accident. It will be the result because you make it happen. Take action and insist on the results you want. They will come! With every experience you share with your children, you are changing and improving how you effectively deal with them.

A Note about Lying

It is upsetting when your children lie to you, but you can help determine whether the behavior continues. As you probably know, lying falls into different categories.

What do you do when your children brag or tell tall tales?

Bragging indicates that children have poor self-esteem, sometimes caused by home, school, or peer pressure. You, as a parent, need to determine if this is the case and take action to lessen your young ones' stress. Tall tales are often told by young children who have not yet defined the difference between reality and fantasy. Creative children sometimes use fantasy to help explain their world. There is no need for concern about this form of "lying." Your children will grow out of this form of lying.

What do you do if your children just tell you what you want to hear? Children who have shared their frustrations, fears, and anxieties with adults and experienced harsh responses will learn not to be truthful and honest. If your youngsters know you expect them to like and do well in school, they're probably not going to share what they think about a particular subject and that they're doing poorly in that subject. "What did you learn in school today" may elicit a "Nothing" response. When you ask your children a question that makes them feel uncomfortable, preface your inquiry with: "I just want to know if you're okay with what happened."

What do you do when your children tell mischievous lies? This doesn't happen often, but some children lie just to see if they can get away with it! Regardless of the reason for the lie, it needs to be addressed. It is effective to say: "I know that is not true," or "It makes me sad when you say things that are not true."

What should you do when your children lie to get out of trouble? One strong motivator to lie is not wanting to experience unpleasant consequences. This is particularly true if the consequences are too harsh or not connected to the behavior. No matter what the category of the lie, you must deal constructively with this challenge. Heim G. Ginott, a child psychologist, stresses that "parents should not be hysterical and moralistic, but factual and realistic. We want our children to learn that there is no need to lie to us."

ENCOURAGE YOUR CHILDREN TO EXPECT A GREAT DEAL OF THEMSELVES

The self-esteem movement of the past decade has taught us some interesting facts: We now know that many children's self-esteem is adequate and in tact. Some youngsters even have an overabundance of self-esteem: those who monopolize a conversation, those who insist that their way is always the best, and those who bully other children. On the other hand, some children's self-esteem needs much nurturing.

It is normal for children from time to time to experience some insecurities, but some young people do need the realization that they are unique and have valuable talents and skills. Young children should be taught early on that they are special. Self-esteem is not only appreciating one's self-worth and importance, but also having the character to be accountable for them to act responsibly toward others. Children's self-esteem may be understood as embracing the feelings and thoughts that individuals possess about their competence and about their abilities to have a positive impact, to confront rather than flee from challenges, to learn from both success and failure, and to treat themselves and others with dignity. Self-esteem directs and motivates our behavior and, in turn, the outcome of these behaviors impacts on our self-esteem so that a dynamic, reciprocal process is continuously in force, playing a significant role in determining whether or not children will become resilient.

Young ones need to be told that they are capable of high academic performance and are expected to achieve this potential in their schoolwork, but always end the conversation with the words: "Try your best." It is a mistake to focus on a particular grade or only on excellent performance on a test. Increasing evidence shows that self-esteem is significantly related to how motivated and successful students are in school. Children experience a sense of genuine accomplishment and satisfaction rather than self-doubt and anxiety about being able to achieve positive outcomes. A student with this confidence level is willing to take risks and learn from, rather than feel defeated, by failure. Concerning academic performance, children will live up to your expectations for them whether or not they come from deprived or affluent environments.

The level of self-esteem is more apparent in some children than in others. Observing how your young ones explore their surroundings and assume control is a way of assessing their self-esteem. How they respond when approaching or being presented with a task is an indication of their sense of competence that will affect the final outcome. To help raise your children's self-esteem, always be positive in your attitude to them. Forgive failure but never be resigned to it. Tell your youngsters that when they do not live up to your expectations you will be disappointed. On the same token, your children should be ensured that when they do well, you will be pleased and proud of their achievement. It is very discouraging for children whose parents are aloof to failures and/or achievements. It is significant to remember that one isolated, recent, but temporary event can influence children's self-concept. Self-esteem, however, should not be judged based on one or two comments that your children make. You can bolster your children's self-esteem in the following ways.

Acknowledge That Your Children Have Value

Listen carefully to what your young ones have to say. Ask questions. Make comments. Help your children identify their own positive strengths. Don't underestimate the power of praise. Compliment your kids often for being helpful and caring. Nothing can replace well-timed, well-chosen words of appreciation. They cost you nothing to give and they are worth so much to your children. Make a conscious effort to ignore minor, inappropriate behaviors. These will change as children grow. Remind yourself to correct your children *privately*. Rather than criticize in negative situations, make rewards available when appropriate behaviors occur. If you are not sure what rewards will be the catalyst for these desired actions, ask your children for ideas. Better yet, give them a choice of one of two rewards. This compensation need not come with a price tag. It could be permission to do something different or to have a few extra minutes of play or perhaps a later bedtime. A hug may be all your children need to encourage an appropriate, desired behavior.

If your young ones are struggling with something, ask: "What can I do to help you?" You might sometimes forget to do this. But remember not to solve their problems. Instead, give your children ownership of their problems and let them figure out how they can facilitate their own solutions.

Tell Your Children That They Are Competent

Provide experiences so that your children can succeed. Offer new challenges and comment on positive attempts. Acknowledge your children's effort toward a goal even if the goal was not attained or reached to your expectations. Give them ideas on how to accomplish tasks. Demonstrate the steps for them. Allow them to carry out and complete the procedure by themselves and remember to supply plenty of practice time if needed.

It is beneficial to acknowledge your children's efforts and the meeting of their expectations rather than to praise a specific task. For example, when your children have completed a task (homework, cleaning up their rooms, taking out the trash, and so on), guide them in their thinking about how the job was carried out. Does it show progress in comparison to how this activity was done previously? In what ways could your children improve it? The goal here is to help your young ones to learn, grow, and make sound decisions with or without others around. They will also feel a sense of self-worth without constant praise and recognition from you or others.

Activities for making your children feel competent

- Give your children jobs: their success with regular chores will help them develop a sense of responsibility and the knowledge that they're contributing to the family.
- Give your children daily or weekly responsibilities, such as feeding pets, taking out the trash, setting the table, or planning or cooking meals. For the children who have difficulty with organization or memory, set out everything they'll need to accomplish their daily or weekly jobs without nagging or frustration.
- Let their teachers know about their special knowledge and expertise. Your children will love knowing more than most adults and will be delighted when their teacher and classmates appreciate their knowledge and ask them questions.
- Let your children lead. Join them in activities that they enjoy and are good at. Computer or video games are areas where they may have more skill than you do. Permit them to show you how far they can progress while you're stuck on level one. Watch what happens! Regardless of the type of game, structure play so they're

likely to win. With each success, you'll see your children gain confidence that will spill over into other areas of their life.

- This one's a no-brainer, but we often forget to do it: Tell your children you *like* them. Give a couple of reasons why.
- Notice changes in personal appearances or in the way your children do something. Use a statement of fact: "The way you're combing your hair is so in style." Statements of fact will be perceived as positive attention even though the change may not be to your personal taste.

Allow Your Children to "Feel in Control"

Provide opportunities for choices, initiative, and autonomy. Try to avoid comparisons among other children. Help your children to evaluate their own feelings and accomplishments. An efficient and effective method for your youngsters to easily come to a decision is to offer them two choices, not three, four, or more. With several choices, children tend to get overloaded and the benefit of the strategy of providing choices is deflected.

When choosing an outfit for school one morning, I showed my son two shirts and said, "Both shirts go nicely with your jeans. Which one would you like to wear?" He made his choice from the limited offerings that I had given him. He felt quite in control of the situation when he chose the brightly colored T-shirt instead of the dark shirt with the collar. Ultimately, the final decision was his! It is often helpful when presenting choices to discuss the pros and cons and/or the cause and effect of the choices with your children to help expedite and clarify their decision making.

Permit Your Children to Be Part of a Peer Group

A very crucial consideration that some parents just don't think about but does wonders for your children's self-esteem is to give permission to take part in kids' activities of the day! Allow your children to more easily "fit in" at school by letting them take part in harmless "fads." Peer acceptance may be just the thing that will give your children's self-esteem a boost. Today, children's successful ability to effectively engage in supportive friendships and peer interactions is central to the development of a positive sense of self.

School-age fads show up in many different ways. These fads change as often as the wind changes direction. Here are some examples: lacing shoes with different colored shoelaces, packing hard-boiled eggs or sardines everyday for lunch, and wearing Hawaiian-style necklaces (both boys and girls). Some parents lack perceptiveness in their knowledge of fads and don't understand how important these fads are to children.

Here is an illustration: Jane liked to wear dresses to school and Nancy, her mother, thought she should wear them everyday. Jane really didn't mind, but all the other girls in her homeroom wore T-shirts and jeans or shorts to school, depending on the weather. Picture day was usually the only "dress day" of the year.

Jane lived in a neighborhood with no children. She didn't have that comfortable group of friends to play with after school. She said that she didn't have any friends at school either. She wanted so badly to make friends. Nancy was concerned but didn't know what to do. At a scheduled parent-teacher conference we discussed some ideas. I pointed out that while there was nothing wrong with wearing dresses to school, Nancy should consider the fact that none of the other girls in Jane's class wore them to school everyday. Jane was not a part of the group! Her style of dressing set her apart from the other girls in the class.

Nancy wasn't aware that the difference in clothes was an issue. That night, she took Jane to the store and bought her several pairs of jeans and shorts. The first, biggest benefit was to know how Jane looked and felt. This little "makeover" worked wonders for her. In addition, she received a lot of positive comments from both teachers and students. Things were also turning around for Jane in the friend department.

Other suggestions for making friends were also discussed at the conference, which included inviting friends over to Jane's home for a Saturday afternoon, going to the movies with some classmates, having a sleepover, going shopping with friends, and so on. All of these suggestions would take a little time to bolster Jane's new attempts at making friends, but the change in wardrobe was an immediate and positive statement of Jane's desire to "fit in" and make friends.

It is safe to say that when you want to make friends during the school years, you have to share and align yourself to others in some visible ways: dress, language, gestures, and so on. For children with questionable self-esteem, changing their style of dress would be worth a try and in the best interest of their making friends. Remember to resist the temptation to impose your concept of "good looking" clothes onto your children.

CREATE AN ATMOSPHERE OF OPEN COMMUNICATION

When is the best time to share the Four Steps to Good Parenting for School Success with your family? Your children want and need your understanding and acceptance. Strive to create an atmosphere of open communication, first by being available just to "listen." The perfect opportunity for sharing is the *family meal* and *family "get-togethers."* Our busy schedules don't often allow us the opportunity of daily mealtimes where we can gather as a family. It is worth the effort that it takes to plan and schedule an occasional family get-together. During these times, include your children in discussions, encourage their participation, and let them know that their opinions are important. The children who are loved and respected for who they are have the greatest chances of enjoying a more balanced self-esteem. Your children's self-esteem will be nurtured in situations when you are not critical and your expectations are realistic. Establishing clear rules, setting limits, and providing your children with opportunities to take responsibility for their own actions is key. All of these methods develop positive feelings and greater self-worth. Encouraging your children to solve their own problems and make decisions will enrich their self-confidence and will contribute to a greater happiness and adjustment not only in school, but also later in life. *What more can we ask for our children?*

Parents need to stay open to listening to their youngsters and, no matter how much they say they don't want your help, understand that they actually do. Remember to teach and not preach. Help them find activities in which they will feel challenged but capable. Show them and tell them they are loved. Point out ways in which they have shown compassion, sensitivity, and care for others.

There are two other approaches that extend beyond family meals and get-togethers that are more formal yet powerful when establishing open lines of communication between you and your children: family meetings and family awards banquets. I know many parents who have successfully used these approaches with their children. They are simply two more effective ways to communicate and build cooperation among family members.

Regular Family Meetings

- Help families feel like a team
- Reinforce trust and respect of each other
- Present opportunities for family members to problem solve
- Involve family members in shared decision making

Things to talk about in family meetings

- Chores
- Television times and program selections
- Phone usage
- Homework
- Play times
- Bedtimes
- Weekend plans
- Vacations

Guidelines for family meetings

1. Meet at a regular time and place
2. Ask family members for a list of their own concerns
3. Write concerns on a posted agenda
4. Let everyone take part in the meeting
5. Give all family members equal time
6. Problem solve and agree on a solution
7. Stick to agreements until the next meeting

Have a Family Awards Banquet

Reward your family with an awards banquet. You can either have it at home or in a restaurant. It's a fun way to recognize family members and to let them know they have done a good job and are appreciated. Before the celebration, ask each family member to write down a special quality or appreciated action on separate three-by-five cards for each member of the family. Present the certificates during dessert or after dinner. You're bound to create a memory for your family they won't forget with a special family awards banquet!

Don't Miss the Bus! in following the Four Steps to Good Parenting for School Success!

Stop! Look! Take Action!

Know and Follow the Four Steps to Good Parenting for School Success

1. Start with a positive attitude.
- Model self-confidence and self-esteem
- Acknowledge your children's strengths
- Role-play to recognize failures and mistakes as "stepping-stones" to success
- Foster family values by your words and actions

2. Create a balance in your life.
- Prioritize what needs to be done
- Tap into your children's interests
- Encourage your children to pursue the things that they like to do
- Create regular family rituals to bring you together as a family
- Use everyday events as learning experiences

3. Remember: You are the boss!

- Establish firm, clear boundaries that leave no doubt that you, as a parent, are in control
- Let your thoughts, words, and actions express limits
- Tell the truth and stand by it
- Focus on your children's needs, not their wants
- Tell your children *what* you expect and *when* you expect it done
- "Put it your way" and firmly
- Give instructions that are direct and concise

4. Encourage your children to expect a great deal of themselves.

- Acknowledge that your children have value
- Tell your children that they are competent
- Allow your children to "feel in control"
- Permit your children to be part of a peer group

5. Create an atmosphere of open communication.

- Call a family meeting
- Have a family awards banquet

In praising or loving a child, we love and praise not that which is, but that which we hope for.

—JOHANN WOLFGANG VON GOETHE

All Aboard!

Strategies for Motivation

○ How can I motivate my children to do their best?

○ How do children learn?

○ What kind of help should I give my youngsters with their homework?

○ How can I help my children prepare for tests?

45

3

KNOW AND EXPLORE THE ROADBLOCKS TO YOUR CHILDREN'S MOTIVATION

Motivation is the key to school success. It is the "why" of learning, the incentive and inducement to move your children to action. Motivation is often defined as the drive that energizes children's behavior toward a goal. Children's incentive comes from two different sources: internally (intrinsic) and externally (extrinsic). The most common problems facing parents during homework sessions and teachers in class work is a lack of this incentive and inducement to effectively and efficiently perform school-related tasks.

Motivation is a general term referring to goal-seeking or need-satisfying behavior. The level or strength of motivation is judged by observing children's attending and persisting behaviors. Student motivation must be taken into account as one attempts to make learning and instruction proceed smoothly. A practical question that must be considered in helping students achieve at learning outcomes is: How can children's attention be gained and focused on learning? Usually, the level of motivation is measured by the teachers' and parents' observations and rating of your children's typical behaviors concerning their schoolwork. There are no good paper-and-pencil tests for this purpose. Evaluation of work samples are useful to infer how well the students attend and persist based on how well they accomplish school-related tasks. Many children seek external reinforcement to motivate their behaviors (e.g., parental approval, good grades, or rewards). Extrinsic motivation often leads to developing intrinsic motivation in your children. Children's motivation often varies depending on the people involved, the setting, what the task is, and, of course, what it involves. The key to developing your children's motivation is to find out what motivates them.

Many things can interfere and lessen children's motivation. The biggest challenges that children have to overcome are fear of failure, desire for attention, "schoolwork is not important" attitude, emotional problems, anger, and lack of challenge.

Fear of Failure

No one likes to make mistakes. Some children are terrified of giving the wrong answer. They don't want to look foolish in front of their teachers, peers, older brothers and sisters, or their parents. Children with a fear of failure will often be observed as quiet, shy, or just the opposite, as "class clowns," engaging in behaviors that mask the real problem. These children rarely answer a question in a class discussion or complete their assignments.

Young children feel incredibly stressed by the many demands they face at home and at school. For them, it's sometimes nerve-wracking work to grow up. It might not occur to your young ones who are stressed out that some of the other children feel the same way. It can even relieve your children's personal pressure to stop and notice that some of their friends also feel anxious and overburdened with chores and schoolwork. In this case, just knowing that others share like burdens will bring them some comfort.

A Note about Shyness Children who are not at ease with other people can overcome their reticence, and the sooner they start working on it, the better for their sense of well-being, academic performance, and, later, professional success. Here are ways to help your youngsters overcome shyness and realize their full potential:

1. Provide direction. You can help your children ease into social situations. Shy children may watch other children playing but not participate, even though they really want to join in the fun. Walk with your young ones to the group and encourage them to say "Hi" and watch a little more at a closer range until they feel comfortable enough to join in the group. Then make a quiet exit.
2. Practice "social reconnaissance." If your young ones are invited to a party or a sleepover, find out who else will

be there. More often than not, if your shy little ones know some of the kids attending, it will make them feel more comfortable.

3. Rehearse an "un-shy" image. Role-play with your children. Rehearse scenes in which they move effortlessly through social settings. Develop a conversational script with them before they attend an event. Help them practice their lines: "Hi, I'm Kyle. Can I join in?" or, simply: "What are you doing? I'd like to play."

4. Promote compliments. The quickest route to social success is by complimenting and encouraging other people. This may be a natural tendency for some shy children because many shy people tend to be sensitive and empathic.

Another factor that comes in the way of intrinsic motivation is the:

Desire for Attention

This is sad, but sometimes true, that some children use poor school success as a way of getting your attention or the teachers' in school. In this fast-paced world, some children who are doing "okay" in school may not perceive that they are getting enough of their parents' attention. These children who previously did everything "right"—got decent grades, completed homework assignments, and did their chores—can feel ignored simply because they are not causing problems. Children who are very dependent on their parents and teachers for their schoolwork and tend to "act out" occasionally see this kind of behavior as a means of getting the attention they need and seek.

I have worked with a *few* children that have a

"Schoolwork Is Not Important" Attitude

Children often tell me that they cannot see how homework and schoolwork relates to everyday life or why it is important. These children need to be reminded that going to school is their "job" and the work that is expected to be completed is their responsibility and part of the job. Adults get rewarded (paychecks, promotions, and awards) for going to work everyday and fulfilling their duties successfully. I believe some type of reward would be helpful when trying to help develop motivation in some children who have this attitude. Discussing the usual transfer of skills learned in school may also help in stimulating your children's inner drives (e.g., adding and subtracting is needed to balance a checkbook, or knowing measurement conversions and reading skills are necessary for putting together a delicious recipe).

Some children cannot focus and attend in class and while doing homework due to

Emotional Problems

Emotional concerns can block the learning process. Depression, frustration, anxiety, fear, or current home problems can interfere with your children's motivation also. Telling the difference between the kids who are depressed and in need of professional help and those who are simply passing through a developmental stage can be very difficult. How can you identify children who may need professional help? Dr. Ed Hammer, a professor of pediatrics and a developmental psychologist at the Texas Tech School of Medicine at Amarillo, says that if children experience one of the following four conditions, chances are that abnormal behavior could point to their being depressed:

1. Living a chaotic life: several moves, divorce, or a parent's frequent job changes
2. Living with a family member who is depressed or having a family history of depression
3. Undergoing a traumatic or painful event
4. Failure to form an attachment to a parent; this may occur in families with alcohol or other drug-related problems

It's important to know what is normal behavior for your children, because kids who are depressed can act either quiet and withdrawn or boisterous and aggressive. According to Dr. Hammer, the key to identifying depression in young people is to look for marked and prolonged changes in behavior. If you suspect these difficulties to be inhibiting your youngsters' school success, it would be beneficial to see your family doctor for a referral to a specialist to help eliminate these patterns that you suspect limit their motivation.

A number of children use schoolwork and their lack of progress as an expression of

Anger

For some reason, young ones exhibit anger toward their parents using their school achievement and behavior as their "control." This is often called a passive-aggressive approach. For example, if children feel pressure to "keep up" academically with their siblings, they may argue with their parents about doing homework or studying for a test—a divergent tactic. This is something within their range of control: poor academic achievement. The more you, as a parent, try to control and structure reinforcement to turn around their behavior, the lower their grades fall.

Only a *small* number of students I have witnessed exhibited a

Lack of Challenge

From time to time, children can be bored with school-work. Students may be "unmotivated" if class work is below their level. In this case, the children are truly not challenged enough and have very little interest in the concepts already learned and the tasks that are assigned. This is a rare occurrence, but one that should be considered when assessing your children's motivational level.

As a parent, you are essential to the development of your children's motivation. You can make a difference in your children's attitude toward schoolwork and encourage their interest and perseverance in tasks pertaining to schoolwork.

Here are some helpful tips to help develop your children's motivation:

- Provide a loving, accepting home environment
- Be concise in your guidance
- Give feedback often
- Set a good example
- Build on your children's nonacademic strengths
- Parallel schoolwork to your children's other interests
- Help your children set goals
- Provide the structure and organization to attain goals
- Offer choices when doing homework
- Emphasize progress made
- Reinforce behaviors that are desired
- Chose rewards with your children that are congruent to their interests

HOW DO CHILDREN LEARN?

This question has been a frequent subject of research for many years. Since the early 1970s, researchers have been studying individual learning styles. They agree that a variety of patterns appear in a typical classroom. Understanding your children's learning styles can help break ineffective homework patterns that cloud your children's learning.

Inefficient homework strategies are ineffective because some children are not getting what they need to learn and fully process information that is presented to them.

Children learn in different ways. To gain a better understanding of how your children learn, consider the four broad areas of preferred learning styles. Each style exhibits very recognizable traits. One of the most popular theories with educators deals with four modes of learning: visual, auditory, kinesthetic, and tactile. These modalities are based on the use of the five senses in the learning process. Which sense the children prefer determines their learning style.

Visual learners best remember what is seen. These children tend to remember faces instead of names, are good readers, and have good imaginations. They respond best to instruction that includes reading, posters, graphs, and videos. Visual learners:

- Take copious notes
- Often close their eyes to visualize and remember
- Are usually neat and clean with carefully coordinated clothing
- Benefit from illustrations and visual presentations
- Are attracted to written or spoken language rich in pictorial imagery
- Seek quiet, passive surroundings

Auditory learners best remember what is heard. These youngsters remember names well, respond easily to phonics instruction, and may like to talk when writing. They benefit most from instruction based on lectures, discussions, and questioning. Some good methods to use with auditory learners include singing songs or listening to tapes that relate to content area to be studied and developing rhymes and mnemonics to help remember information. Auditory learners:

- Remember names, tend to forget faces
- May not coordinate clothes but can explain what they have on and why
- Hum or talk to themselves
- Enjoy listening to themselves and others
- Like to read aloud
- Remember best by verbalizing
- Have difficulties reading maps or diagrams
- Have little trouble learning in a noisy environment

Kinesthetic learners learn best by doing, experimenting, and being involved. These learners remember what was done, not necessarily what was seen or heard, and might have difficulty paying attention and staying focused on their schoolwork or homework. Kinesthetic learners benefit most from hands-on instruction, using manipulatives, role-playing, or building things. Kinesthetic learners:

- Need to move around, be active, and take frequent breaks
- Speak with their hands and with gestures

- Seek out and find ways to move around
- Tinker when bored
- Rely on what they can directly experience or perform
- Enjoy manipulating materials

Tactile learners like to use their hands and fingers to learn. These children learn best by writing, drawing, and doodling and tend to be creative. They benefit from instructions such as sewing, painting, or drawing. Tactile learners:

- Need to touch or feel objects when learning a new concept
- Enjoy designing things
- Like to illustrate written work
- Find sculpting, painting, and drawing relaxing
- Appreciate physically expressed encouragement (e.g., a pat on the back)

As the learning style theory suggests, students have a predominant learning mode followed by their second, third, and fourth preferred style. Knowing and understanding your children's preferred learning style is useful to you when you tackle homework assignments with your children. Using this "multisensory" or "multimodal" approach to learning when helping your children with their homework assignments will stimulate and enhance your children's learning processes. It will surely increase your young ones' academic success. Using a multisensory or multimodal learning style approach, you will change the pattern of failure to success and meet the needs of your children who are academically "at-risk." Using this approach will empower you to reach your children's learning preference even if it is not always clearly defined.

Children struggle when they try to learn in ways that aren't natural for them. When you plan a variety of demonstrations of instruction, your children can utilize their individual strengths to succeed in school. Remember, there is never "one" right way or an "only" way to teach and help your children with their homework. Helping your children with their homework in the future, coupled with the knowledge of the various learning style preferences and the use of technology, will add a new dimension to your pursuit of successfully meeting your children's learning needs. With your creativity, knowledge, and motivation you will meet the challenge.

IDENTIFY AND PRACTICE HOMEWORK TIPS

Homework accounts for one-fifth of the time that successful students are engaged in academic tasks. Also, many children both in regular and special education classes have homework problems. What is needed are some coping skills to deal with their homework woes from time to time. The main problem lies in the fact that the teachers assign the tasks to be completed at home in an environment over which they have no control. We all recognize that aspects of family life influence students' homework outcomes. Homework is a unique opportunity for you to share in your children's success in school, personal growth, and future learning. It is a chance for you to participate on a daily basis and to let your children know that you care and believe in their potential.

Your children's ability to be successful with homework assignments begins with the value you place on responsibility, effort, and hard work. Success also requires helping your children develop essential homework strategies and developing a working alliance with your children and their teachers. Completing homework assignments is a challenge to say the least for both students and parents. It doesn't have to be a frightening experience if you have a plan.

Homework has been a part of the U.S. education since the beginning of the nineteenth century. What is the role of homework in your children's learning process? Teachers sometimes depend on it to complete unfinished class work, give additional practice, and, most importantly, to keep parents informed of their children's progress. Teachers and parents believe that doing homework helps students take responsibility for themselves and develops personal management skills. If you are like most parents, you feel mixed emotions about homework. Even in well-functioning families under ideal circumstances, homework can be one of the biggest contributors to a parent-child crisis. If you are like most parents, you feel a mixture of emotions about homework. Some of them are positive, but many of them unpleasant. You can turn these negative feelings into positive ones by following these proven approaches and methods.

1. Adapting the Home Physical Environment Is Foremost in Establishing Homework Success

Choose an appropriate place Where homework will be done (in the children's rooms, at the kitchen table, or in a quiet corner in the family room) is as important to its successful completion as the academic skills needed. A designated homework area provides the framework for an environment that will reduce poor organizational habits and procrastination.

Gain consensus All family members must first come to an agreement on the value of homework. Set a certain place and time for assignments to be done without distractions (pets, video games, television, and friends). Gaining this consensus establishes an atmosphere conducive to sustained effort.

Develop a routine Consistency is a vital element in learning processes, especially for children who need structure. A set homework time helps in establishing the value of homework by putting it on your regular schedule and sticking to it. This customary schedule over time becomes a habit—"just the way we do things around here"—and is not questioned or disputed. Frustration, annoyance, boredom, confusion, and even anger are the many negative emotions, you as well as your children, express when it comes to homework. Most of us did not like homework when we were kids and probably don't like it any better as parents, but it is a fact of life! The sooner we adjust our attitude and the homework environment, the closer we come to schoolwork satisfaction.

Create a homework checklist Design a homework checklist or poster that is easily accessible and in clear view in
the designated "homework place." Answers to the following questions will give a quick review as to the quality and
the thoroughness of homework assignments. *Refer to it
before, during, and after an assignment is complete:*

☐ Is your name and date on the paper?
☐ Did you follow all the directions?
☐ Is your work neat and your handwriting readable?
☐ Does each sentence begin with a capital letter?
☐ Do other important words need capital letters?
☐ Does each sentence end with the correct punctuation?
☐ Is each word spelled correctly?
☐ Is each sentence a complete thought?

For math-related assignments, add the following questions:

☐ Did I choose the correct operations for word problems?
☐ Did I complete all the steps?
☐ Are my numbers legible?
☐ Are my numbers aligned in the proper placement
(number under number)?

This strategy may seem a bit cumbersome, at first. Yes,
it will take some extra time, but in no time at all it will
become second nature and part of the learning process on
which your children will come to rely. How quickly you'll
see results. In just a few minutes every week you'll power

up your kids' potential, sharpen their skills, and help them stay ahead of the homework game.

Put up a "Do Not Disturb" sign Your children can decorate it as they wish. Hang it up in a prominent spot where all can see. This visual cue emphasizes the seriousness and importance of the task at hand.

Supply a homework survival kit Fill the kit with desk supplies. Have it in the "homework place" ready and waiting at your children's fingertips.

2. Identify Tasks That Your Children Can Do Independently

The manner in which you will check over the completed work also needs to be established. After the independent assignments are finished, help your children tackle the work that needs your assistance. Not everyone works equally well with a particular child. If neither parent or older siblings can work effectively with your children, then perhaps a tutor is needed. It is important for all concerned that the relationship established during the homework time should be given strong consideration.

Do easiest work first Start with the work that your children can do independently. This will build confidence and set the tone for the particular homework session.

Use association techniques Address the nonmastered skills assignments by associating the material with something that is known: "If you can spell 'book,' try to spell 'cook'—just change the first letter," or "two thousand pounds equals one ton; a compact car weighs about two thousand pounds." Use math knowledge to solve real-life problems: "How much gas did we use on our last car trip?" "What percent of our weekly food money goes to snacks?" or "Think of a candy bar divided in six pieces. Would you like to have one of the six pieces (one-sixth) of it or five pieces (five-sixths)? Apply the relationships of problems like these to the skills needed to complete the assignment.

Be in close proximity to your children while they're doing their homework, even if they choose to do it alone. Some children will need a parent sitting right next to them. Some will need you to read over the directions with them. Make sure that they understand and follow them. You wouldn't believe how many children's homework assignments are done wrong and turned in without their parents' signature on them. Students' assignments are usually done wrong not because the children lack skills but because of distractions, other priorities, or just passive involvement at best. As your children get more proficient at the "homework game" and more confident in their own abilities, your proximity to them may be lessened gradually.

Set goals for homework completion Set goals and use a clock or timer to help your youngsters develop a sense of timeliness for required tasks. Encourage your children to take responsibility for their homework. Don't allow yourself to get trapped in lengthy discussions or arguments.

3. Give Direction and Guidance for More Difficult Tasks

When your youngsters don't seem to grasp a concept that is so apparent to you, frustration mounts. If this happens, try some of the following tips.

Separate text from graphics Direct your children to look over pictures, charts, or graphs before reading. Visual cues can sometimes provide information that is needed to answer questions even before reading the text.

Use analogies When doing math problems, make up a short list of steps to help remember all the procedures that need to be done and in what order. For example, when your children are working with division problems, write "DMSB" or "*Dad, Mother, Sister, Brother*" on top of their paper to help them remember the steps in long division problems: divide, multiply, subtract, and bring down.

Reverse roles Try reversing roles when doing homework. Play the role of the student and have your children play the role of the teacher. Explaining concepts to others is one of the best ways of learning concepts.

If the tug of wills during homework involves "normal stress" for you, tell your children: "It is just something you have to do." However, if it is truly negatively affecting your parent-child relationship, it's time to get yourself out of the mix and seek some help. Some suggestions that work for parents are using a neighbor, high school student, or a paid tutor who offers homework support. You and your children will be the better and happier for it if you can't seem to work well together.

4. Accept Responses As Genuine Effort

We all don't work on full capacity twenty-four hours a day, seven days a week. Your children, who appear to be lazy, may be just tired from a busy day. Poor handwriting may be the result of having no lines on the paper or perhaps not enough space for the answer. If your young ones are tired or frustrated by the length of the assignment, you could alternate reading paragraphs on the page with them. In math or spelling assignments, alternate working on math problems. Say to your child: "You do the odd numbered ones and I'll do the even numbered ones. We'll be done in no time at all." If you use this approach only once, it is in the best interest of all concerned to speak with your child's teacher concerning frustration level and the length of the assignment. Ask the teacher to modify and reduce the number of problems. In the case of the child not grasping the concept, ask that the skill be retaught and how you may assist the reinforcement of this skill at home.

Adapt and Modify Homework Processes and Procedures

Be creative! The benefits of adapting and modifying homework procedures far out weigh disciplining your children. Keep the tempo upbeat. Remember, the goal of homework is to fine-tune skills by practice. New approaches offer fresh alternatives for learning and growth. Even young kids come up with novel and original observations. They should be encouraged to be imaginative and adventuresome in their thinking and to express themselves in their own words. Nothing could be more discouraging to a small child than to come to a parent with some discovery or revelation, only to be met by indifference. When young children bring you questions or want to share their insights, listen with interest. You need not applaud every idea or even agree with it, but you should treat your independent thinkers with genuine respect.

Express Affirmation for Diligence Let your children know what you think of their effort and hard work for diligence and creativity during a homework session. Give affirmations such as: "Your ideas in this paragraph show lots of imagination!" or "You really stuck with it. You finished it so quickly. You did a great job!"

5. Focus on the Goal of the Assignment

Often, a social studies, math, or science homework activity can turn into a remedial reading lesson. Keep in mind the focus of the assignment and do not let poor skills in reading, spelling, and math interfere with the intended goal of the lesson. By telling your children an unknown word or numeral, you are permitting your youngster to gain knowledge or locate an answer rather than teaching reading mechanics. In this way, you are fostering a possible liking for social studies, math, or science rather than a dislike of reading.

A Note about Parents *Doing* Homework! Does this really happen, you ask? *Yes it does!* Although you would not use this technique to help your children, don't even entertain the thought of doing your children's homework for them. Out of desperation and frustration, some parents do complete their children's homework assignments. (If you ever get to this point, at least write the answers on another piece of paper then have your children copy your answers onto the original homework paper.) If you do your children's homework for them, what message are you really giving them? Think about that for awhile! The best solution is to write a short note to the teacher, tell him or her of the previous night's situation, and ask for an extension on the assignment. Most understanding teachers will accommodate this request if it doesn't happen too often.

6. Use a Homework Planner or Assignment Notebook

To help your children acquire the necessary organizational skills, a homework planner or assignment notebook may be exactly what your children need. Many students need to be shown how to use the planner/notebook. Demonstrate where and how to write homework assignments, perhaps using abbreviations. When the assignments are finished, put a check mark next to the work that is completed. Even a better idea would be to sign your initials next to the checked-off finished work. It would be helpful to teachers if you would also write a short message as to how well the children did on the tasks during the homework session. Many teachers will comment back to you as to their evaluation or with some insightful tips for future homework completion.

If by chance nothing is written in the planner/notebook, instruct your children to call a friend. Keep a list of classmates' phone numbers to contact them in case clarification is needed. If handwriting in the planner is illegible or if assignments are not recorded on a consistent basis, notify your children's teachers of the problem. They surely will have some suggestions for you.

Showing students how to graph their homework completion is a powerful strategy. This feedback is just what some children need to help them stay on track. I have used this strategy with my students and it is really an eye opener to both children and their parents. Students used green magic markers to record completed assignments, yellow for late assignments, and red for assignments that were either incomplete or not turned in. Yellow would become green or red depending on each student's follow-up. A simpler variation of this method works just as well. Students put a green, yellow, or red dot in the homework assignment book next to the assignment. In both instances, many red dots speak loud and clear to all—students, parents, and teachers—about the children's consistent failure to complete homework. Green dots are always a cause for celebration. You might want to consider a reward for weekly homework completion (all green dots). Ask your children to select a possible treat, such as renting a particular home video, eating at a favorite restaurant, or getting more play time. Rewards can be small treats, but they go a long way in defining schoolwork as important.

Even if homework is not assigned on a particular day, sign the planner/notebook anyway. Get into a habit of doing so. Consistency in this matter may be just the thing that will turn your kids' homework woes into happier times. Write short notes to the teacher about how well your youngsters are doing. If you check your children's planners/notebooks daily, you won't have to complain at parent-teacher conference time or when you receive their report cards that you are unaware that your children are doing badly. Signing the planners/notebooks and exchanging short notes with teachers are frequently effective in alerting to both parents and teachers the children who are experiencing problems. Early warnings allow time to address problems before it is too late in the school year.

Use a calendar or chart If needed, use calendars or charts as extensions of the planners/notebooks to organize your young ones' weekly schedules: chores to be done, dates of tests, baseball practices, or Scout meetings. This way they'll know what to expect each week. There won't be any surprises.

Check contents of backpacks before children go to school
Check with your children at night or in the morning after homework is done to make sure that everything (books, binders, homework, planners/notebooks, and so on) are in their backpacks and ready for the new day at school. Homework requires a set of skills that oftentimes are not directly taught by teachers. Yet, these skills involved in completing homework successfully, such as time management and organizational strategies, are important well beyond the school years and need to be taught both in school and at home!

Adults continue to seek methods to improve their skills, often at considerable personal cost. You, as a parent, along with your children's teachers, can do much to help students assume responsibility for their own learning and to acquire these basic, lifelong skills. With patience, insight, and an action plan, you can avoid "missing the bus" this year and help your children experience homework success. Show your added interest by reviewing your children's textbooks so that you know what they're learning in school by planning family activities that relate to their studies.

7. Know Your Children's Teachers

The homework issue should not be whether children should or should not be helped with homework but rather how to assist them. Sometimes, knowing the teachers and coaching your kids to respond to the teachers' values is more important than advising the teachers of your children's needs. All of us have sought assistance in our out-of-school assignments and your children are no different.

For children to learn good study skills, teachers and parents must work together. It is most important to help children build good habits, to develop a system that works for each child, and to use the system effectively and consistently. Preferred learning styles vary from child to child. Children need to discover, with both the parents' and the teachers' input, how they learn and then work out a study system that works best for them. Use homework completion suggestions from the teachers to teach organization skills and to improve study skills. Remember that the primary purpose of working together with your children's teachers is to improve your children's overall learning and to foster good work habits.

"Meet the Teacher" night at the beginning of each new school year is a great way to gain a clear understanding of the expectations, rules, and standards regarding homework. Ask the teachers in what subjects they plan to assign homework, how much, and approximately how long assignments should likely take. Some schools even supply a homework manual for your reference. If you're one of the fortunate ones to have this benefit, refer to it often.

Ask for further testing If a discrepancy arises between your kids' homework performance and the teachers' expectations, discuss alternatives with the teachers. As a parent, you can be part of the solution by providing descriptions concerning what happens at home during homework time. Sometimes, the solution requires that the teachers adapt assignments to the students' capabilities. If the teachers cannot give you a clear and understandable answer as to why your children are experiencing difficulties in school and in doing homework, ask for some basic testing that the school provides. This is your right and above all the right of your children. If the amount or difficulty of the assigned work does not match your children's abilities, it is your duty to speak with the teachers to modify and adjust their expectations.

8. Time-Management Considerations

Time management really means managing your self! It is a way to be happier, more efficient, and more effective. It is a strategy that your children will need to succeed in school and throughout life. It enables your youngsters to:

- Lead a more balanced life
- Have more free time
- Meet deadlines
- Achieve more

The best benefit of learning time-management skills is that your children avoid spending time on things that are unimportant. With your help, they can be on their way to time-management balance when they:

1. Make a list of things to do on paper.
2. Divide the list into two parts: fixed commitments (homework) and flexible commitments (free time and having friends over).
3. Complete tasks that they must do at certain times (school, sleep, meals, and appointments).
4. Assign priorities. Number items accordingly.
5. Update the list. Cross off items as they do them. Add new ones.
6. Make up a schedule. Pick the best times to work and play. This puts them in charge of their time!
7. Look at the schedule. Use the schedule. Follow it. Make time work for them!
8. Monitor and adjust.

TEST-TAKING TECHNIQUES

Tests are a part of school life much too the dismay of most students. Many of these children can handle the time management needed and the overall pressure of taking tests. Some students are mentally and sometimes physically overloaded at just the thought of a test-taking situation. In many cases like this, tests do not accurately measure your children's true knowledge of the subject and their ability to learn, process, and remember information. There are many ways to help your young ones work smarter and not harder and to "ace" any test-taking situation. Reduce the worry about tests and improve test performance and outcomes. Here are some practical ways that you can take the fear and anxiety out of test-taking situations:

Before the Test

Use a study guide If your children's teachers do not usually provide study guides, ask them if they would consider doing so. If the response is not positive, you can design your own for your children by following these various tips.

1. Write down the main ideas of a science or social studies chapter on a three-by-five index card. Memorize them!
2. Jot down incomplete sentences. Instruct your child to fill in the blanks. Write in the answers. Memorize main ideas!
3. Define key vocabulary words from the lesson or story. Write down short, concise word meanings. Memorize each one!

It is more important that your young ones concentrate on major, focal ideas than spending time on details that may be irrelevant. Reading, studying, and memorizing the major items of a selected lesson will always produce a better grade when taking a test. Don't cram. In the week before the test, schedule shorter study sessions. Your children will feel less pressure and they'll remember more.

Be a good listener Remind your children to be good listeners and follow test directions. In the primary grades, test directions are given both orally and in writing. Stress to your children that if they don't understand the directions the first time, they should ask their teachers for clearer directions. It's better to be safe than sorry later. Tests in elementary school are usually not timed and even if they do have a time limit it is advisable for your children to take the extra minutes needed to be sure that they are on the right track for a successful test-taking situation by understanding the directions.

Get a good night's sleep Your children getting plenty of sleep the night before a test is the second best preparation for test taking, other than lots of study, study, and more study!

Eat a good breakfast Don't underestimate the power of a good breakfast. Some children don't want to eat so early in the morning and that's okay. In that case, send a snack with them to be eaten on the bus or in the homeroom before the test or at recess. If they really don't want the snack before the test, surely they'll enjoy it after the fact—when most of the test anxiety is over.

"Always do your best" Emphasize to your young ones to do their best on the test. It is a mistake to put qualifiers on your expectations. Say: "Always do your best," instead of "Bring me an A+" or "I know you'll get a 100 percent." You lessen the pressure for your children if you follow this simple rule.

During the Test

Read the directions Usually, teachers will read and explain the test directions with the class. If they don't, remind your children to read the directions and remember to ask for clarification if they don't understand them.

Skim the test quickly This test-taking strategy is much overlooked by students. Many times when students complete the short, easier sections of the test, they gain more confidence. They can then continue the test with less pressure. By skimming over the test, your children will know what to expect and can pace themselves a little better for a longer or written essay section of the test.

Skip hard questions Tell your youngsters not to be afraid to skip a question on the test. It is better for your young ones to skip a question that they're unfamiliar with or one that is too hard than wasting time on it. Their score will be better if they complete accurately the items with which they're most familiar within the time limit of the test. If there's time, they can always come back to try the harder questions toward the end of the test.

Check over work Remind your children to make sure that they didn't skip any part of the test. This happens often. When the test is turned in, it's a little too late to make corrections or complete missed sections. If there's time, check over for correct spelling, punctuation, capitalization, and grammar. In a math test, always check the signs (operation of the problem) and note careless mistakes, such as adding instead of subtracting, which can lower the test grade substantially.

After the Test

No test can measure a child's worth! Here are some things to tell your children to put taking tests into perspective:

> "One test is only part of your grade. What is most important is that you have an understanding of the subject. One poor test score will not equal to a failure grade of your report card. Your attendance, attitude, daily work, and of course homework make up your final or report card grade."
>
> "You'll do better next time. The subject and interest level will be different."
>
> "Let's try and figure out what will help you do better next time."
>
> "Tests are stressful situations. Let's talk about how you can better control the circumstances and your feelings."

Above all, inject humor into your conversation with your children. Increase family laughter. Show that life can be joyful and fun—even after a test that didn't go so well!

A Note about Standardized Tests

Standardized tests help measure your children's progress. Their results are compared with those kids at the same grade level nationwide. Schools also use the scores to see what areas of the curriculum may need to be strengthened. These tests usually cover many different subject areas and are often impossible to study for. Doing home-work regularly is one of the best ways your children can prepare. Also, you can share these test-taking tips:

- Pay careful attention to the directions
- Spend about the same amount of time on each question
- Check your answers and make sure the answers match the right questions when using a separate answer sheet

A good night's sleep the night before and a healthy break-fast on test day can help too!

Don't Miss the Bus! in recognizing and practicing Strategies for Motivation.

Stop! Look! Take Action!

Recognize and Practice the Strategies for Motivation

1. Know and explore the roadblocks to your children's motivation.

- Fear of failure
- Desire for attention

- "Schoolwork is not important" attitude
- Emotional problems
- Anger
- Lack of challenge

2. How do children learn?
- Visual learning style
- Auditory learning style
- Kinesthetic learning style
- Tactile learning style

3. Identify and practice homework tips.

Adapting the home physical environment is foremost in establishing homework success

- Chose an appropriate place
- Gain consensus
- Develop a routine
- Create a homework checklist
- Put up a "Do Not Disturb" sign
- Supply a homework survival kit

Identify tasks that your children can do independently

- Do easiest work first
- Use association techniques
- Set goals for homework completion

Give direction and guidance for more difficult tasks

- Separate text from graphics
- Use analogies
- Reverse roles

Accept responses as genuine effort

- Adapt and modify homework processes and procedures
- Express affirmation for diligence

Focus on the goal of the assignment

- Remember that social studies, science, or math assignments are not remedial reading lessons

Use a homework planner or assignment notebook

- Refer to a calendar or homework chart for more organization
- Check contents of your children's backpacks before they go to school

Know your children's teachers

- Ask you children's teachers how best to assist with homework
- Work together with your children's teachers about homework concerns
- Attend "Meet the Teacher" night
- Use the school's homework manual, if available
- When homework problems persist, ask for further testing

Time-management considerations

- Learn time-management skills
- Manage time, manage yourself, and manage your children

4. Test-taking tips:

Before the test

- Use a study guide
- Be a good listener

- Get a good night's sleep
- Eat a good breakfast
- "Always do your best"

During the test

- Read the directions
- Skim the test quickly
- Skip hard questions
- Check over your work
- If there is time, go back to the hard questions

After the test

- Remember, no test can measure a child's worth!

> *To know how to suggest is the*
> *great art of teaching.*
>
> —HENRI-FREDERIC AMIEL

Buckle up, Stay in Your Seat!

Discipline without Tears

○ Why do my children behave the way they do?

○ How can I get my children to listen?

○ How can I help my young ones express their anger in a nonvolatile way?

○ What strategies do I need to assist my youngsters in resolving conflict?

UNDERSTAND THE REASONS BEHIND
MOST CHILDREN'S BEHAVIOR

Just reacting to your children's misbehavior is usually too little, too late, and rarely does anything from preventing these behaviors in the future; however, there is good news! Being proactive and following an action plan of strategies can prevent your children's negative behavior in the first place. To be successful in this new approach to help you control your children's negative responses, you will need a step-by-step method. It's likely that your current methods are actually working against you and what you want to accomplish.

What is it that you want for your children? Do you want them to think on their own, to make decisions, to take initiative, and to recognize choices and their consequences? Children are much easier to "like" and "deal with" and "less stressful" to be around when they do what we want. The big question is what is the payoff for them? Docile, obedient children are often motivated externally by disapproval, criticism, or fear of punishment. Other children are well behaved and motivated by internal, personal needs that are not dependent on others. How do you bring them to this point?

If your current discipline approach stresses self-management and personal responsibility, outcomes are not enough. Don't settle for children's externally motivated actions. The cost to your children is too high. These children make their decisions based on other's needs. Complying and pleasing you is a source of recognition and approval, but it only teaches them that they are worthwhile when they are doing what someone else wants. We say to ourselves that we don't want this to happen, but sometimes even our best intentions and seemingly harmless words and actions reinforce exactly that.

You can expect your children to cooperate with you, but before that you need to decide what you can reasonably expect from them. Each child is a unique mix of talents and behaviors. Some of these will never change. Some traits may grow, some will lessen a bit, but they probably won't go away because of developmental stages, temperament, heredity, and environment. Remember, your children's behavior always has a purpose. You've probably asked yourself many times: "Why do my children misbehave?"

There is a reason behind most children's behavior. Children want to feel accepted and to belong. When kids can't or don't belong with positive behavior, they find out that misbehavior is a payoff for them. Your children, believe it or not, whether consciously or subconsciously, have a goal for their misbehavior.

Are Your Children Attention Seekers?

If children believe that they can't get attention in a useful way, they seek it by misbehaving by doing something annoying (e.g., kicking a table leg, screaming, or interrupting). Some children seek attention in a much different way: by doing nothing (e.g., dinner is ready and on the table and your children are still watching television even after several reminders). Even though your children are not "acting out," this type of misbehavior is a cry for attention.

Parent Strategies for Attention Seekers

- Ignore annoying behavior. Don't say anything. Try not to look or act upset in anyway.
- Give your children choices: "You can watch television quietly or go out side and play. You decide."
- If choices don't work, do mention consequences: "Please do something constructive while I'm on the phone or you may not use the phone for the rest of the night."

Are Your Children Control Seekers?

When children feel that the only way for them to belong is to be the "boss," they are seeking control of a situation.

These kids want to control not only the circumstances, but they also desire to control their parents, such as by yelling at them ("You can't make me do it!") or by throwing a tantrum. Usually, the relationship between parents and children in this situation is the escalation of the misbehavior, so the parents get angry and fight back. A cycle then exists that seems to never end, but if they do give in, the children's behavior stops.

A Note about Back Talk Back talk is a sure sign that something is amiss in your relationship with your youngsters. Proper communication is the key to remedy this very annoying habit. Sometimes, children are dealing with some unsettling issues and just don't know how to tell their parents or ask for help. Whatever its cause, back talk is disrespectful to you, as a parent. If your children talk back to you and get away with it, you send a message that it is okay to be disrespectful to you and other adults.

Act quickly and consistently when your children talk back to you. Say: "Back talk is not allowed." It's important not to empower your young ones by arguing about the issue that triggered it. Put it your way and firmly: "That's the way it is," or "I will not tolerate back talk." If your children are chronic back talkers, you've got your work cut out for you now. Say to your kids: "From now on, back talk will not be tolerated." To reinforce your conviction, present a list of consequences that will occur if the back talk continues. Most importantly, be ready to follow through with them. You will defeat the whole purpose of disciplining your children if you back down from following through on the consequences that you set or change them in any way. You must be specific, concise, and serious when dealing with a back talker. With consistent and loving effort, the back talk will lessen and in time will be erased. You will be doing your children a huge favor if you help them control their back talk. Can you imagine how back talk will affect their life at school and in later life at work?

Parent Strategies for Control Seekers

- Be silent at first, then say it your way and firmly
- Follow through on your list of consequences
- Leave the room or the situation
- Do not try to confront your children
- Engage in another activity

Are Your Children Get-Even Seekers?

Usually, children who seek revenge, after losing a power struggle with the parents, want to get even with them. Children may say or do something that is both hurtful and harmful, such as by being rude or saying untrue things about the parent. The result is often an ongoing "war" between the parents and the children.

Parent Strategies for Get-Even Seekers

- Refuse to comment or fight
- Simply ignore the incident
- Talk with your children when everyone is calm

Are Your Children Giving-up Seekers?

Sometimes, children give up trying when something is hard for them, such as schoolwork or sports. It is usually an area in which the children feel unable to succeed. When children give up, the parents feel like giving up also. When this happens, the children's goals are met: the parents have agreed to expect nothing from their children.

Strategies for Giving-up Seekers

- Be careful not to pity your children.
- Encourage your children with your words and actions.
- Go to their sports events and say: "Wow! What a great catch! I know you could do it."
- Go to your children's school activities. You might consider saying: "Your story and illustration are the best!" or "I really enjoyed reading your assignment and thought your picture was perfect for the story."

ESTABLISH DISCIPLINE WITHOUT TEARS!

For your children who are in need of some behavior interventions, consider applying Discipline without Tears!, a proactive discipline approach that has its basis in a "win-win" philosophy. The focus is that everyone's (parents' and children's, and perhaps even a third party's) needs are considered. All concerned feel valued. This proactive approach is effective because it is grounded in the belief that children resist being controlled. In trying just to "control" your children, you use an inordinate amount of time and energy. This type of reactive control takes away their opportunities to develop confidence, responsibility, and self-control.

Develop a win-win discipline approach with Discipline without Tears! using the strategies that will help prevent most discipline problems before they occur. Discover the six steps of this highly effective discipline and behavior expectations plan. Create a home environment that encourages appropriate behavior and decreases repeated misbehaviors. Learn positive, highly effective ways to deal with inappropriate behaviors. Develop and maintain an efficient and effective discipline that works for you and your children. Most of all, maintain dignity for you and your children in your approach to disciplining your young ones. The following six steps will help you establish, teach, and consistently implement effective rules. Each step has a positive impact on your children's behavior and lets them know that you have their best interest in mind.

The Discipline without Tears! approach will foster high levels of your children's behavior at home that will result in improved academic behavior in school.

Step #1: Separate Your Children from the Action

Separating your youngsters from the action is basic if you are to effectively handle the negative behavior without attacking their worth. Say to the child: "I love you, but I don't like you hitting your sister." Many times, you think you send clear messages to your children but you really don't. In some cases, your children just weren't listening or maybe they didn't process your directions in the manner you thought they should. In some situations, you may need to set new limits, options, or sometimes even consequences.

An appropriate strategy is needed because different situations call for different responses. For example, you tell your children: "Clean up your room." You remind them of this chore over and over again. In your mind, you have a set time and a procedure for them to respond to your request, but often your "good time" is not in their "good time." Clarification of the time limits to this request need to be made at this point.

You will get a better response to your appeal if you say: "Clean up your room after your homework is done," or "Take the trash out before dinner." When being more specific in your instructions, the job that you want to get done or the certain behavior you would like to be displayed will more likely be an outcome in the time limit you desire. If this doesn't work, think about establishing a more effective motivation or consequence. Express to your youngsters: "When you're finished cleaning up your room, after dinner we'll go out for ice cream," or "You may call a friend after you take out the trash." Use whatever rewards that will work with your children. You know your youngsters better than anyone. You know what will work best to motivate them. If you're not sure, ask them what would be a motivating reward for them. Remember to take mental notes.

Step #2: Give Positive Reinforcement

Parents often try to illicit a behavior from a child by praising another sibling. Keep in mind that positive feedback is best used to maintain and reinforce desired existing behavior, not to change a behavior. Some praise and positive feedback for your children when they do something worth recognizing is in order at this point. Give the recognition in straightforward terms. The goal of positive reinforcement is to let you start with and build on positive behaviors. A positive focus will change a child's perceived threat into a much desirable promise. It's much more effective in influencing your children's behavior if you communicate this to them: "As soon as you finish your lunch, we'll watch a video." Rather than: "If you don't finish your lunch, you won't watch the video." A promise is much more respectful and pleasant to hear and is much more likely to get a positive response from your children than making a threat, no matter what the situation may be.

Use recognition as a very effective response to your children's progress to good behavior. When you recognize your young ones' positive behavior, an alternative to praising, it neither depends on your approval, nor does it establish value judgment on the children. Recognition simply describes young ones' behavior and offers no value judgment. Recognition statements help connect your children's behavior to how it pays off for them. It will be effective to say: "Your homework is complete, now you may go out to play." Recognition focuses on the task itself and its benefit to your children—not on you!

Step #3: Motivate by Giving Choices

Motivation is also important because children choose options based on what will fulfill their needs at a given time. Some children may be motivated by getting a dollar for an A on their report card. Maybe letting your children choose meaningful outcomes—payoffs for their choices or for what they do—will be more beneficial.

Having choices often generates cooperation and commitment when threats and bribes haven't worked. For example, your child has three homework assignments. Try offering your youngster some options. Ask your child to select the sequence of the assignments to be completed. Set some limits and options (not too many) to help your young one make good choices. You don't want to overwhelm and confuse a positive situation by offering too many options. Two choices are sufficient to make this strategy work effectively.

My primary school students have enjoyed a story entitled "I Can't Get My Turtle to Move." No matter what the little boy in the story does, he can't get his pet turtle to "come alive" and walk over to him. He tries many things to get the turtle to move. None of them work except at the end of the story when he waves a piece of lettuce in front of the turtle's shell. Only then does the turtle poke its head out of its shell and take a few steps toward the boy—toward the lettuce. After trying many things to entice the turtle to move, the little boy finally stumbles on what motivates the turtle.

I have often used this story line in discussing negative behaviors and discipline problems with parents. I don't want to imply that this technique of using food, a primary reinforcement, as a reward is so simplistic or that food works as a motivator every time. You do need, from time to time, to troubleshoot to find out what "works" with your children. I didn't say that this approach to discipline is always fast and effective the first time around in every given situation, but it is a good starting point to alter your children's negative behaviors to more positive ones.

Step #4: Connect Choices with Outcomes

Both positive and negative consequences build responsibility by helping your children connect choices with outcomes. As long as your children stay within the limits you impose, they experience positive consequences. A negative result is a lack of access to the desired outcome. Remember, consequences teach more than words. As long as consequences are made clear ahead of time, it is in your children's best interest to allow them to occur. Following through on clear limits and options is a good positive reinforcement.

James, a very responsible nine year old, is diligent about avoiding foods to which he is allergic. He does not like to feel out of control, which is what happens when he eats any food containing a red dye additive. His mom says that when she reminds him about the bad feeling he gets when he ingests anything with the dye, it is the best motivator for him. The reminder, alone, keeps James away from the harmful dye better than any consequence his mother could have come up with for him.

Another important consideration is to set limits for your children according to their age and personality. Have your children outgrown the limits you set for them? Many parents never realize the importance of checking if the limits they set are still appropriate. Bedtimes, rules about talking on the phone, watching television, playing video games, and seeing friends need to be changed as your children mature. Many times and within the same family, you may have to modify and adjust things a little differently for each child. "My daughter is talkative and outgoing and I always try to set her boundaries more closely," a father of one of my students expressed. "My son is so shy that I experiment with boundaries that stretch him a little." If you relax a boundary and your children don't respond positively, you can always return to the way things were. You can approach them in this way: "We tried letting you set your own time for cleaning up your room on Saturday but you haven't cleaned it in two weeks. You have to go back to the old rule of cleaning it up after breakfast. We can try again in a few months."

Some families review the limits they set with their children at the beginning of each school year and make adjustments. If you haven't made any changes in your family's rules for awhile, now might be a great opportunity to do so. Have you ever tried the "write" rule? If your children don't take rules seriously, try putting the rules in writing. On a piece of paper or in a notebook, include the rules and what happens if they are disobeyed. You may jot down in the rule book: "Put your bike and skateboard in the garage when you come inside for the evening. They will not be returned for three days if they're left outside overnight."

Step #5: Develop a Work Ethic in Your Children

Give your children small jobs to perform, not only the care of their own possessions, but also tasks that serve the entire family. Even very young children can put their clothes away, get the mail, or set the table. These kinds of responsibilities give children a feeling of independence as well as a sense of their own worth. Youngsters who learn to accept the discipline of daily duties early in life will be more likely to accept the discipline of school more readily and complete their responsibilities without question. Children who are brought up to accept no responsibilities will certainly look on schoolwork as an unreasonable imposition on their time and energy.

The work ethic, which has always been a strong element in American character, seems to have disappeared from school as well as the workplace. Part of the fault lies with parents, but you can reverse this attitude. Help your young ones understand that for the rest of their life they will be expected to perform some tasks that are neither enjoyable nor self-fulfilling. They must be taught that significant achievement is almost always the result of hard work. This idea may be the single most important element in the dynamic growth of your children at home, in school, and in the world of the Information Age.

Step #6: Set a Good Example

As a parent, you have the responsibility to behave in such a way that your young ones can look up to you and learn from your actions. Of course, you need to instruct and guide them with your advice, but receiving only the right instruction will make little or no difference to children who see parents and other adults doing the very things they have warned them against doing.

If parents say they value reading and then spend all of their time playing videos games, then children will inevitably come to the conclusion that reading is not really worth while after all. Children understand, sometimes better than adults, that "actions do speak louder than words." Good behavior begins at home. As a parent, you can help your children become well adjusted and self-disciplined. Concerning your children's behavior, school success depends on your cooperation with your children's teachers in enforcing the school's discipline policies. You can be a major part of your children's educational development if you consider the following tips to guide your children to school behavior success.

SEVEN EFFECTIVE WAYS TO INFLUENCE YOUR CHILDREN'S SUCCESSFUL SCHOOL BEHAVIOR

1. Ask for a Code of Conduct Manual. Most schools have them. Help your children become familiar with school rules and regulations and support them.

2. Take an active interest in your children's academic and extracurricular activities.
3. Discuss your children's behavior patterns with their teachers.
4. Find out why your children are misbehaving. Talk with your children and be a active listener.
5. Stress the importance of good discipline to your children.
6. Monitor your children's behavior and adjust your strategies at home by encouraging the discussion of daily events.
7. Show respect for your children and they will show respect for you and for others in return.

Another consideration that children need to understand is the importance of being considerate of others, whether at play or at school. Many academic problems can be traced to social difficulties. Socially well-adjusted children are more likely to be successful students. Young children should be exposed to larger groups whenever possible: at church, community centers, and at functions where they can participate in activities with people other than their immediate family. These types of environments present good opportunities to practice courtesy and respect toward others. This lesson is among the most crucial your children can learn in preparation for school, where they will be involved for an entire day with both children and adults who come from different kinds of homes and backgrounds.

HELP YOUR CHILDREN EXPRESS ANGER

One of the problems with school-age children today is their inability to see the long-term benefits of discipline and hard work. As a consequence, they give up on their studies and concentrate of things that are not as important. They often consistently voice negative feelings, make inappropriate choices, and express their anger in different ways that are both inconsiderate and annoying to others. There is good news, though. You, as a parent, can channel your children's angry outbursts in the following ways.

Some children turn to anger when they feel they can't endure some distressing situation. Usually, these kids lack the skills for expressing their feelings of anger. *These tips will help you recognize and help your children who are withdrawing or exploding over everyday frustrations.*

- Listen to what your children are saying about their feelings and be willing to talk about any subject. Some young children are dealing with some adult issues, but their minds and bodies are not developed enough to handle these stresses. Don't "boil over" with personal reactions. Say to your children: "You may have a point, but let's look at the facts together and discuss them."
- Provide comfort and assurance. Tell your children you care about their problems and show confidence in their ability to handle them.

- Tell your children that everyone experiences anger and that it's okay to sometimes feel angry. Try to assess the source of the anger by asking questions. Develop a clear picture of outcomes and communicate them to your children. Say to your children: "If you do this, that will happen," or "Your friend doesn't know how you feel. Why don't you tell her?" Help set up a meeting if needed.

- Encourage your youngsters to shift gears and engage in some positive activity to help refocus thoughts and alleviate angry feelings. Maintain a consistent focus regardless of your children's demands and pressures. Ask them: "How would you feel if your friend did this to you?" or "Would you like to be treated like you're treating your friend?"

- Teach basic problem-solving skills for use with this and future situations. Then let your young ones use these skills to figure out a solution on their own.

- Talk over the steps to rectify the situation together. Role-play if necessary. Look at how you handle your anger. Are you setting a good example for your children?

- Acknowledge good behavior. Take every opportunity to reinforce your children's healthy response to anger. Mention improvements in behavior that you have observed.

A Note about Bullying

The first- and second-graders at the Elm Street bus stop were being bullied by Sam, a fifth-grade boy. Apparently,

Sam got in trouble for forcing the smaller kids out of the rear seats of the bus every morning. His father was furious when he found out and wanted to ground him for a year. Sam's principal had a better idea. She gave him a choice: "Sit in your assigned seat or sit in the seat directly behind the bus driver." This wasn't a hard choice for Sam to make. He soon got over his need to sit in the back of the bus. He eventually became friendlier and more protective of the little children at his bus stop.

Methods of bullying Both boys and girls bully others, but they do it differently, according to results from the

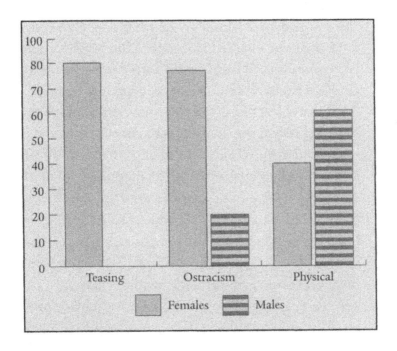

Midwest Bullying Studies conducted by the Bureau of Educational Services and Applied Research at the University of North Dakota (see graph on previous page).

If your children's angry behavior continues, consult your children's school guidance counselor or psychologist for more needed information and helpful resources.

HELP YOUR CHILDREN RESOLVE CONFLICT

You, as a parent, can develop an action plan for your children to resolve conflict. Modify them to suit your individual parenting style.

1. Recognize and acknowledge the problem. Determine the real problem. Think about what is really wrong. Does everyone involved understand the problem? Did you communicate your expectations clearly? Perhaps a simple misunderstanding is at the root of the problem.
2. Defuse a disruptive or volatile situation. Perhaps the most important step in defusing a conflict situation is to move to a neutral location. Talking out a problem can be an effective way to diffuse an emotional situation.
3. Establish an open and positive atmosphere. Stay in control of your emotions, set ground rules, and do not place blame. Once you have neutralized the situation, you are ready to begin negotiating a solution. Everyone involved should agree to abide by these rules.
4. Ask questions and listen carefully. Assemble the facts from all sides without judging. When each person involved

speaks, the others should listen without interrupting. Then each person can ask questions of one another. When you believe you have enough information, it is time to reverse the roles. You speak and the others listen.

5. Determine the effect. How does the conflict affect those concerned? Consider how each individual feels. Make suggestions to make the situation better. No one's feelings or beliefs should be brushed aside; that action will only create more conflict in the future.

6. Find some common interest. When everyone agrees on one point, it can be the foundation of some resolutions. Make some agreement, even if the agreement is to disagree. You might want to start by agreeing that everyone involved wants the best for everyone, even though you have different ideas about how to achieve that goal.

7. Discuss possible solutions and negotiate to develop a win-win solution. Develop a workable plan with suggestions from all sides. It is important for everyone involved to make a personal commitment to support the plan they developed. (Adapted from "Nine Steps to Conflict Management," *Strategies* [February 1996])

Follow these simple steps the next time a conflict arises. You may be surprised how well they work!

Four Ways to Fix It Quick!: Children's Mini-lesson

If you're angry . . .
If someone else is mad . . .
If you think there may be a fight . . .

1. Walk away: If someone else is fighting mad, just walk away. No one can make you fight.
2. Share: Do you both want the same thing? Sharing is a great way to avoid an argument or fight.
3. Talk it out: You don't have to argue. Just talk about it. See what you can work out together.
4. Say you're sorry: If you did something that upset someone and you feel badly about it, just say you're sorry. A lot of times that makes the other person feel better and you will too.

The Discipline without Tears! strategies will open many doors for you and your children, doors to the joys of parenting and the wonders of childhood. If you realize that you cannot "reach" your youngsters and modify their negative behavior, seek professional advice from your family doctor, psychologist, or counselor. When children continually "act out," even after all your interventions, they are telling you that they need more than you can give them. Remember to seek professional help when needed. You and your children deserve the best!

Discipline without Tears! is a cooperative, win-win approach, but it is not a magic act. It is a process that often involves rethinking your goals and modifying and adjusting your ideas and actions. Developing a cooperative relationship with your children takes time, patience, and, above all, faith in yourself and your children. It may be difficult for you, from time to time, but *Don't Miss the Bus!* Buckle up, stay in your seat! Guide your children to good behavior at home and school. Your children are worth the effort!

Don't Miss the Bus! Take advantage of Discipline without Tears!

Stop! Look! Take Action!

Rely on Discipline without Tears!

1. Understand the reasons behind most children's behavior.

Is your child

- An attention seeker?
- A control seeker?
- A get-even seeker?
- A giving-up seeker?

2. Establish Discipline without Tears!

Step #1: Separate your children from the action—communicate clear, specific instructions

Step #2: Give positive reinforcement—communicate recognition in straightforward terms

Step #3: Motivate by giving choices—communicate clear consequences ahead of time

Step #4: Connect choices with outcomes—communicate clear consequences ahead of time

Step #5: Develop a work ethic in your children—give your children small jobs to perform

Step #6: Set a good example—remember "actions speak louder than words"

3. Effective ways to influence your children's successful school behavior:
- Know and practice the Seven Ways to Influence Successful School Behavior
    1. Ask for a school Code of Conduct Manual
    2. Take an active interest in your children's school activities
    3. Discuss behavior patterns with your children's teachers
    4. Find out why your children are misbehaving
    5. Stress the importance of good behavior to your children
    6. Monitor your children's behavior and adjust your interventions
    7. Above all, show respect for your children

4. Help your children express anger.
- Recognize how to help your children who are withdrawing or exploding over everyday frustrations
- Listen to what your children are saying about their feelings
- Provide comfort and assurance
- Tell your children it's okay to feel angry

- Encourage positive activity
- Problem solve with your children
- Acknowledge good behavior

5. Help your children resolve conflict.
   - Recognize and acknowledge the problem
   - Defuse a volatile situation
   - Establish an open and positive atmosphere
   - Ask questions and listen carefully
   - Determine the effect
   - Find some common interest
   - Discuss possible solutions

Four ways to fix it quick!: Children's Mini-lesson

- Walk away
- Share
- Talk it out
- Say you're sorry

Instruction increases inborn worth, and right discipline strengthens the heart.

—HORACE

BUS STOP #5

Watch the Signs: Learning Along the Way!

Effective Home-School Partnerships and Parent-Teacher Conferences

○ Why is the home-school partnership so vital for my children?

○ What is my part in the home-school partnership?

○ How can I get the most out of parent-teacher conferences?

○ How does volunteering "pay well"?

5

HOME-SCHOOL PARTNERSHIPS

Often, educators find parents who, rather than accepting their role as partners with educators in an effort to cultivate well-adjusted, well-educated, next-generation leaders, fall short of their responsibility. Without doing their "part," they come into school with a "my children—right or wrong" attitude. Educators report parents say things like: "I can't make him read" or "I can't control who her friends are." At home, these parents are friends and equals to their children. They hope that this "good relationship" with their children will be enough to keep their children "on track," but it seldom seems to happen that way. Unable to balance what is done with what needs to be done in a home learning environment, these parents are puzzled when their children have problems in school. They are surprised when they are unable to balance friendships with discipline and set limits in after-school life at home.

Think of the Teacher As a Partner

The following are some tips for creating a good relationship with your children's teachers.

1. Make contact early in the school year Attend "Meet the Teacher" night or set up a meeting early in the new school year. Introduce yourself to your children's teachers in the first few weeks of school. If problems arise later, you'll find it easier to talk with them after a positive, first meeting.

2. Create a positive attitude Like parents, teachers need to feel appreciated for the job they do. Don't focus only on the negative, point out the positive of your children's school experiences also. Call or write the teachers to offer your thanks for their concern, thoughtfulness, time, and effort spent on your children. You'll brighten their day and strengthen your partnership. They will be encouraged and more readily to share good news about your youngsters' progress in school.

3. Keep the teachers informed Let the teachers know about important changes in your children's life that might affect their academic performance and behavior. Include any new medical conditions and changes in medication, and above all changes in circumstances at home. Remember, wise partners don't look for blame when problems arise. Working together as partners does make a difference in the students' life. This relationship offers your children the support and consistency that is needed for success in school. As partners, together you will find solutions that will benefit your children at home, school, and throughout life. At no time in the history of America has the need for successful home-school partnerships been more important. Most school personnel will freely admit that the increase in success of the current public school system hinges on the supportive relationship between parents and schools. Make a special effort to support school authorities and to remind your children to be respectful of them. Make certain, rather than guess, whether your children are contributing to any classroom chaos. Too often, school conflicts center on incidents involving respect for peers and situations involving property rights: notebooks, pencils, clothing, and sometimes even food. Respect for other's property also means refraining from destructive behavior, including acts that deface or destroy schoolbooks, classroom walls, lockers, and hallways. It is your responsibility to make certain that your children have a strong sense of property rights of other students. It is the basis of this respect and trust that is needed in any future good relationship.

CREATE AN EFFECTIVE PARENT-TEACHER CONFERENCE

A parent-teacher conferences are important because they can help your children succeed in school. The better you and the teachers work together, the more your children will benefit. It is a great way to show your children you care. When you show an interest in your children's school life and offer them a strong support system, they will:

- Have a positive attitude toward learning and school
- Feel proud of their achievements
- Enjoy school more

It is important for parents to prepare for the conference and help set its tone. Conference time is limited, so go well prepared.

Before the Conference

- Talk to your child to find out if there is anything you should know before talking to the teacher.
- Review your child's progress: report cards, progress updates, and work sent home for your review. Note your child's special talents as well as areas of difficulty.
- Note a change in family circumstances and routine that may be affecting your young one's behavior.
- Make a list of questions and concerns. Don't rely on your memory. Decide what you want to tell the teacher. It will be invaluable information to the teacher for you to include a report of what the child is saying at home about school.
- Get a baby-sitter for younger children. I can't tell you how many parent-teacher conferences have been

unproductive because the parent as well as the teacher were distracted by the behavior of a younger sibling. Do yourself a favor by securing a baby-sitter for a parent-teacher conference. The rewards will outweigh any inconvenience.

During the Conference

- Make sure the teacher knows what it is you want to tell him or her and what you want the teacher to tell you about your child. Some ideas for information that you might want to gather from the teacher or share with him or her include: social adjustment, progress in academic and nonacademic subjects, your child's standing in a group, and of course your youngster's relationships with adults in authority.

- Give priority to areas of special concern and raise only the issues that seem most important to you and your child. The parent-teacher conference is not the time and place for a "general dissatisfaction with the school" discussion. You'd do better scheduling a special conference in which your own concerns and not your child's will be the focus.

- Find out from the teacher what you can do to help your kid meet the school's expectations and goals for him or her. Create a climate of partnering with the teacher through acknowledgment of the teacher's work with your child.

Make the most of your conference

- Arrive on time
- Listen carefully
- Ask questions
- Stay calm
- Raise important concerns first
- Be direct
- Develop an action plan for future school success
- Thank the teacher for his or her concern, time, and effort
- Stay in contact with your child's teacher

After the Conference

- Involve your child by sharing your parent-teacher discussion with him or her
- Volunteer to help in the school
- Remind yourself that what happens after the conference is just as important as the meeting itself
- Stay in touch with your child's teacher

Both parents and teachers want their children to succeed in school. Parent-teacher conferences are an important tool for ensuring your youngsters' achievement. Through regular conferences, parents and teachers share what they know about the children in their charge, allowing both to accomplish more than either can accomplish alone. Parent-teacher conferences also improve the relations between the home and school. They provide an opportunity for teachers to explain the curriculum and acquaint parents with the objectives of the school. School achievement occurs when parents are involved in a support system with the children's school and are informed and kept up to date on their young ones' academic and social progress. Parent-teacher conferences are an essential instrument in the education process: There is no other procedure that is as effective for bringing parents and teachers together for the benefit of the children. These regularly scheduled meetings are a chance for both parties to voice their own concerns. If the teachers really listen to the parents, they can learn much that will help their students. If you, as a parent, are involved in formulating solutions to any problems your children may be experiencing, the results can be extraordinary for them. Another extension of the home-school partnership is to take advantage of parenting classes given in your school or district. Parenting classes are a great source of support. Join a parenting group to build your skills and confidence. As you do, you will become a better and more knowledgeable parent. Working with your children will become easier. It also gives you a chance to get to know your children's administrators and school staff. Many parents report that the affirmation given in the classes shows that the things they are already doing with their kids are "right." Parenting classes also give you the opportunity to listen to other parents' advice. One mom in particular shared that she, as a manager of other people in her job, was able to use many of the techniques learned in parenting classes in her position at work. Some of the methods she employed at her work were acknowledging the problem, noting other people's perceptions and emotions, clearly conveying everyone's thought processes, and proceeding to a solution that was a mutual agreement. She also emphasized that she received useful information that could be applied in adult situations while attending the parenting classes at her children's school.

VOLUNTEERING PAYS WELL!

Volunteering at your children's school is a wonderful way for you, as a parent, to connect with other parents. While it keeps you in touch with your children's teachers and school activities, it is a way to enhance your own personal and educational growth. The benefits are significant! By volunteering you will:

- Meet other parents who share concern for their children's school success
- Encounter a variety of viewpoints and outlooks
- Observe how other parents deal with problems and adversity
- Gain new skills
- Think differently about your problems

There are countless ways you can help your children's school. Here are some ideas:

- Share your work, hobbies, and travels with students
- Volunteer as a library aide
- Read your favorite children's stories to your children's classes
- Help out in the school office, computer lab, or lunchroom
- Support fund-raisers for school computers and playground equipment
- Make school grounds more attractive
- Serve as an officer in the local parent-teacher organization
- Volunteer as a room mother or father
- Go with classes on field trips

THE IMPORTANCE OF THE
HOME-SCHOOL CONNECTION

Teachers spend more time in your children's waking life than you do during the school year. Some teachers even think of themselves as surrogate parents. It is important for you to recognize and appreciate the impact that teachers and the school environment have on your children's development. It is imperative that you collaborate with your children's teachers in the quest for school success. As in any partnership, tensions may surface at anytime, given differing expectations and goals for your children. An effective parent-teacher partnership does not suggest that differences of opinion will not arise from time to time. As in every good relationship, respect and trust are crucial. In airing these differences and focusing on the growth of well-being in your children, these tensions can be managed and lead to positive outcomes through problem-solving methods.

Have you ever wondered why "Meet the Teacher" night came into being? The rationale for these meetings is that they encourage a positive start to the new school year. If it wasn't for "Meet the Teacher" night, usually the first contact teachers have with parents or vice versa is when children are experiencing problems. If this is the case, a negative or defensive tone is set for the year. This first meeting with your children's teachers is a great opportunity to set the groundwork for the year ahead so that you and your children's teachers can work positively for the benefit of your children. Teachers want you to know that you have an open invitation to be an active participant in your children's education.

The contact that you made at the beginning of the new school year must be maintained throughout the year. Usually, schools send out newsletters, bulletins, and flyers to parents informing them of class and school activities. Progress reports in the form of interim notices and/or report cards are sent home quarterly. Teachers may spotlight your children's competencies in short notes from time to time. Showcase these recognitions in some way to celebrate your youngsters' success. A favorite place of honor to display any good news in our house was (and still is) our refrigerator. A parent recently shared with me that the

display of his awards, good report cards, and other com-
mendations placed on the refrigerator by his parents
helped his self-esteem greatly. He said that he continued
this tradition when he got married, but his wife wasn't that
fond of the clutter on the refrigerator door; so he bought a
refrigerator for the garage and continued to put his "good
news" items on that refrigerator door! Old habits die hard!

Any little display of recognition of your children's
achievements means more to them than they'll ever say to
you. My son just recently received his MBA with honors
from a well-known university. When his final grades were
mailed to him, he placed his grade report on the refrigerator door. And now, after two months, they're still there
reminding him, his dad, and me of his dedication, perseverance, and excellence in the pursuit of his goals.

Ongoing communication between home and school is
crucial when your children have learning or social difficulties. More frequent contact with your children's teachers is
typically necessary and serves as a preventive measure. For
children in need of life-skills support, daily journaling may
be required. With my students in need of organizational
skills development, I usually write notes to the parents in
these children's homework assignment books. In turn, the
parents comment back to me as necessary to help keep
their children on track with responsibilities.

When your children are having ongoing setbacks in
school, you and your children's teachers must expend
increasing time, effort, and energy to ensure positive outcomes for the children. If the parent-teacher connection

wanes, your children will be the ones who are most affected. If your young one has a teacher who is less friendly and supportive than his or her teacher from the previous year, you may have to work a little harder and more earnestly to develop a working relationship for the benefit of your child. Be patient and empathic and persevere for your child's sake so that his or her problems are successfully addressed and lessened.

Sometimes, your own anger, fears, and anxieties can become roadblocks to the resolution of the problems your children are experiencing. It is not unusual from time to time for teachers to sometimes be less than tactful in the way they attempt to share information about your children. It can most frequently illicit anger, resentment, and defensiveness in you. In the following three scenarios, effective solutions are thwarted:

- At a parent-teacher team conference I attended, Alice's communication arts teacher began the conference by sharing Alice's three-sentence story that was filled with capitalization, spelling, and punctuation mistakes. This presentation was followed by examples of the same story idea that were done by Alice's classmates, complete with illustrations. She concluded the exhibition with the comment: "I've been teaching for a long time and have never seen so many mistakes in a short story before. Alice clearly has *lots of problems.*" Without a doubt, Mr. and Mrs. Hughes, Alice's parent, were taken back and upset with the manner in which they were informed of Alice's lack of mastered skills. Needless to say, the meeting took a downward spiral from that point forward. The teacher didn't even so much as offer any suggestions as to how Alice could improve her written expression skills at home or in school.

- Parents, sometimes unknowingly, can also affect the positive outcomes of an initial parent-teacher conference. Mrs. Taylor approached her son's teacher and blurted out: "Carl doesn't want to come to school this year. He says you don't like him and he doesn't like you!" The teacher reacted: "The way he acts in school, he's a hard child to like!" The conference was over, no matter what was discussed after that initial comment.

- During another parent-teacher conference I sat in on, the teacher often used the terms "auditory processing skills," "visual-motor coordination," and "multimodal cues." Both parents attending the conference were confused as to the meaning of the terms used by the teacher. Even after the meanings of the terms were explained, Eric's mom still wasn't clear about what they denoted but was afraid to ask again for further clarification.

If you, as a parent, are to be an essential part in the home-school connection, you need not to be fearful to ask the right questions and reask them if necessary. It is most important that you and your children's teachers are "on the same page" understanding and implementing the strategies that will facilitate your children's learning process. Once you agree on the skills and the techniques to follow, you must have a backup plan if some of the strategies that you put in place are not working. If a strategy isn't effective, parents and teachers alike can learn from this seeming setback rather than feel defeated by the lack of immediate success. Remember to modify and adjust procedures as necessary.

Parents, please remember to be empathic to your children's teachers. Try to communicate your information in a manner that encourages the teachers to listen and act accordingly to what you have to share. I give this same advice to teachers: to be positive and respectful when conveying that your children may be experiencing difficulties in school so that the problems may be assessed and positive solutions be put in place to help your youngsters' skill remediation. Throughout my teaching career and in my consultation to educators, I have experienced firsthand the benefits that accumulate when parents and school personnel work together as partners. Continued cooperation and effective communication are vital in helping young ones develop the skills necessary to achieve both social and academic success. Another positive aspect of the home-school connection is to get your children involved in the planning for their journey to school success. Having your young ones involved in the "game plan" to facilitate their own remediation nurtures a sense of involvement and ownership—perhaps the missing key in the ever so important home-school connection. When parents, teachers, and the children in their charge work as partners with respect and trust, this relationship will yield not only advantages at home and school, but also lifelong benefits for the children in their care. Truly, your children are the "precious cargo" that must be handled correctly and positively if they are to be successful on their journey to school success!

Don't Miss the Bus! when it comes to the home-school connection!

Stop! Look! Take Action!

Establish Positive Home-School Partnerships

1. **Think of teachers as partners.** Create an effective home-school connection. As a parent, you have an open invitation to be an active participant in your children's journey to school success.
   - Make contact early in the school year
   - Nurture a positive attitude
   - Keep teachers informed of changes

2. **Create an effective parent-teacher conference.**

Before the conference
- Review your child's progress
- Note changes in family circumstances
- Make a list of questions and concerns
- Get a baby-sitter for younger siblings

During the conference
- Share information with the teacher
- Give priority to areas of special concern
- Ask the teacher how you can help your child

After the conference
- Involve your child by sharing your parent-teacher discussion
- Volunteer to help in your child's school
- Stay in touch with the teacher during the school year

3. **Remember that volunteering at your children's school pays well.**
- Meet other parents
- Encounter a variety of viewpoints
- Learn how others deal with problems
- Gain new skills
- Think differently about your problems and your children's difficulties

4. **Showcase your children's competencies and achievements in some way and in a place of honor.**

5. Establish ongoing (daily if needed) communication with school personnel when your children have been diagnosed with moderate to significant learning or social difficulties.

6. Be patient and empathetic with your children's teachers for your children's sake.

7. Ask for clarification of terms and strategies in parent-teacher conferences; ask again and again until you are sure of your vital role in the home-school connection.

8. Collaborate with your children's teachers to create a backup plan if current strategies aren't working.

9. Learn from setbacks in your children's progress, and modify and adjust procedures when necessary.

10. Communicate with school personnel in a positive and respectful manner.

11. Involve your children in the "game plan" for their own skill remediation.

> *Knowledge is a treasure,*
> *but practice is the key to it.*
> —THOMAS FULLER

Destination: Arrival at School Success!

Every Child Is Special in Some Way

○ How smart are my children or should the question be: How are my children smart?

○ What are Gardener's eight types of intelligence?

○ How are my children special?

EMPHASIZE THAT YOUR CHILDREN
ARE SPECIAL IN SOME WAY

If your children are not A+ students that's okay. It's more important that kids find something that they're interested in and in which they are competent. When your kids' interests are captured, they work hard to develop their skills and what's more important they "stick with it."

As a young boy, my brother was very interested in car racing. He knew the names of the best racers, he read books about racing, and faithfully followed race results. In relation to this interest in car racing, he was showing some enterprise, and so much so to my mother's dismay. One summer day the lawn needed to be cut, but he couldn't cut it with our lawnmower! Earlier that day, Mike removed its motor to power his newly constructed go-cart! He also shared an enthusiasm about fire fighting. One day he was driving me to an appointment but we were delayed a few minutes because we followed a fire truck on its way to a fire. My brother was very disappointed when we and the firemen got to the destination. It was a false alarm! My brother has since moved on to a successful executive position and is still passionate about car racing (he has a lot of trophies for his "wins") and fire fighting. In addition to his corporate job, he is now a volunteer fireman and a licensed emergency medical technician.

I think a good reason to worry is if your children aren't engaged in any constructive activities. It may even be your fault in some cases. When children see examples around them of people engaged in wholesome experiences, setting a good example is the best teaching method. Even though these activities chosen by your children wouldn't be number one on your list of things to do, your children are learning to connect with the world in their own way. Each child is unique and special in some way. Help them to find activities that they like and that best suit them.

A Note about Downtime

Baseball teams, soccer leagues, tutors, dance classes, horseback riding, homework, and so on and so on. . . . The lives of our children are as overscheduled as ours are! Sometimes, parents have to "schedule" unscheduled time for their children. Remember, we are trying to strive for balance in our lives. These unscheduled, "doing nothing" times are actually when most kids do their best thinking and when creativity comes in play. Consider these questions: Are all these enrichment activities good for your overscheduled kids? Do your children really want and like to do these particular activities or are they the activities that interested you in your youth? Be honest. Assess your children's motivation and your own.

If your children's life is overscheduled and if downtime cannot be included during the school year, why not consider the summertime and holidays for a chance to include it and take a new direction with your kids. Try saying to them: "Go out and play!" See what happens. Give them a chance to be left to their own devices so they can manage their own free time. You'll be delightfully surprised at their creativity and ingenuity.

Giving your children a break from organized activities and electronic baby-sitters could very well mean that they will be bored—at first! Child development experts say that when deprived of anything else to do, children will find a way to amuse themselves—even if it means simply daydreaming. That's exactly the point: letting your youngsters use their own creativity to fill some of their time. In the process, they will be giving a workout to their mental, emotional, and social skills. "Empty hours" teach children how to create their own happiness. Children need adults in their lives who understand the relationship between boredom and creativity—and are willing to set the stage so that kids can create and play. You might provide materials (e.g., magic markers, colored pencils, or a dry erase board and pens) and even gentle suggestions if necessary. One thing you need to remember, however, is that your role isn't one of camp director. Constructively bored kids eventually turn to a book, build with Legos, use paints to create a "masterpiece," or perhaps get in a game of baseball in the neighborhood. Your children need your guidance if their downtime is to be constructive and lead to creativity.

Most of today's parents learned the benefits of creative play as children. Left to your own amusements, you found resources that you didn't know you had. You learned valuable lessons from your creative play, but I'm not so sure that your busy, overscheduled children will have the chance to learn them. Inventiveness and self-reliance are being scheduled right out of them. Child development specialists acknowledge that finding time for unstructured play isn't easy. It's particularly difficult for single parents and for families that live in rough neighborhoods where playing outside isn't the first option. The benefits of unstructured play are so great that parents are encouraged to try to find at least one hour a week for it. The following tips will help make getting started a little easier.

Limit television Most experts say this is the most important recommendation, and admit that it's probably the most difficult, both for the children who will pout and for their parents who use television to give themselves a breather. Studies show that children watch an average of thirty-eight hours a week; cutting back on the amount of television can free a good-sized chunk of time for unstructured play.

Limit other "screen" time Most children spend hours each day in front of computers, hand-held video games, or watching videos in the minivan. Set a daily time limit for your children to be "unplugged" and left to their own devices within reason.

Choose toys carefully Increasing unstructured play time doesn't require a big investment in new toys. Some basic art supplies, library books, and objects collected from nature (e.g., leaves, pinecones, and acorns) can keep your kids busy for quite some time. The value of a toy is proportional to the degree that it invites imagination and creativity. Consider the story of two girls: Jean and Joan were comparing notes about their dolls. Jean had an electronically enhanced doll and boasted: "My doll can say one thousand words! Joan quickly held up her old-fashioned doll and replied: "My doll can say anything I want her to say!"

Send your children outside to play Playing outside promotes more running, which helps your children sleep better at night and battles obesity. Make sure that your children are going outside for recess during school time. Like adults, children need a break from their work.

A study on fourth graders compared students who had recess with those who didn't. The children who didn't have recess were more fidgety and less on task for their classroom activities.

Spend time watching your children play It is not necessary for you, as a parent, to join in your children's play. You can sometimes partake in your young ones' creative play, but be careful not to "take over." A highly successful strategy is to involve yourself spending time each day with your children doing whatever they choose to do. During this "special time," your children make the decisions, control the flow of the play, and assign roles. It's unstructured play time for your children, yet you get to participate. Designing some special time with your children almost forces you to slow down, to alter the rhythm of your daily schedule in order to make time for them. Given your other obligations and the length of your to-do lists, it is all too easy to forget the good stuff, namely how much you actually like your own kids as people, how much you enjoy their company, and how important it is for you to connect with them and have fun together.

HOW ARE MY CHILDREN SMART?

Yes! Every child is special in some way. Intelligence is not a single, dimensional, unchanging, easily measurable quality. We don't always look at enough variables in determining exactly what our children need and exactly how they are unique. The intelligence quotient (IQ) score used by school psychologists measures only two (verbal and mathematical) of the eight types of intelligence identified by Howard Gardener, a Harvard researcher and psychologist.

The essence of Gardener's Multiple Intelligences (MI) Theory is to respect the many differences among children, the multiple variations in the ways that they learn, and the numerous ways in which they can leave a mark on the world. In his theory, Gardener seeks to broaden the scope of human potential beyond the confines of the IQ score. He suggests that intelligence has more to do with a capacity for solving problems and creating products and services in a context-rich and naturalistic setting.

Key points of the MI Theory

1. Each child possesses all eight intelligences
2. Most children can develop each of the eight intelligences to an adequate level of competency given appropriate encouragement, enrichment, and instruction
3. Intelligences usually work together
4. There are many ways to be intelligent within each category

MI Theory emphasizes the rich diversity of ways in which children show their gifts within and between intelligences. What about the other six types of intelligence? According to Gardener, individuals don't have one fixed intelligence but at least eight distinct ones that can be developed over time. These eight kinds of intelligence are listed with some activities to stimulate each type of intelligence.

Verbal/Linguistic (involves ease with reading and writing skills)

Play word games or language-oriented ones (Scrabble, Spill and Spell, and so on) or crossword puzzles.

Choose your favorite movie or television program and write a sequel or tell what you think will happen in the next episode or in next year's series.

Logical/Mathematical (the ability to reason deductively or inductively and to recognize and manipulate abstract patterns and relationships)

Select a project requiring you to follow directions (assemble a model airplane or bake cookies).

Visual/Spatial (the ability to visualize shapes in three dimensions)

Express yourself. Share your ideas, opinions, and feelings with different media (magic markers, oil paints, play dough, and so on). Plan a scavenger hunt with friends. Draw a secret map with many details and the location of the treasure for all players.

Intrapersonal/Introspective (the ability to understand oneself and be aware of inner feelings, intentions, and goals)

Keep a journal. Record key events from your day. Express your feelings about the events. Reflect on them. Evaluate your thinking strategies and patterns you use in different situations. Develop alternate plans for any given situation.

Interpersonal/Social (the ability to get along well with others and to work with them effectively)

Try to guess what others are thinking and feeling. Experiment with supposing an individual's profession, background, or talents just by observing nonverbal cues (dress, accent, and gestures).

Bodily/Kinesthetic Intelligence (the ability that involves the body to solve problems, create products, and convey ideas and emotions)

Express your mood by various activities (dance, jog, or walk). Try role-playing to express an idea or opinion of feeling. Play a game of charades.

Musical/Rhythmic Intelligence (the ability to be sensitive to rhythm, pitch of sounds, and responsiveness to music)

Experiment expressing your feelings in relationship to a favorite song. Listen to and learn from the sounds and rhythms in your surrounding the environment (e.g., rain on a window, the air conditioner, or traffic).

Naturalist Intelligence (the ability to recognize and classify numerous species—the flora and fauna—of an individual's environment)

Research topics of great interest (e.g., cloud formations, mountains, volcanoes, or whales).

According to Gardener, the question should not be: "How smart are my children?" but "How are my children smart?" Gardener's ideas focus on the fact that the eight types of intelligence can de developed and nurtured. His premise is not meant to be a way of pigeonholing students into set categories. For children to develop these eight intelligences, parents and teachers need to perceive children as having a combination of these intelligences and being capable of growing in all of them.

As a parent, you must never loose sight of the fact that each of your children, no matter how they are special, must have an environment where they can thrive and succeed. These eight intelligences must be nurtured by

Intelligence	Strong In	Likes To	Learns Best	High-End States	Misbehaviors
Verbal/ Linguistic	Reading, writing, telling stories, memorizing dates	Brainstorm, read, write, tell stories, talk, memorize, keep a journal	Reading, hearing, and seeing words; speaking, writing, being in discussions	Martin Luther King Jr., T. S. Elliot, Maya Angelou, Abraham Lincoln	Passing notes, reading during lessons
Logical/ Mathematical	Math, reasoning, logic, problem solving, patterns	Solve problems, question, reason, work with numbers, experiment, use computers	Working with patterns and relationships, classifying, abstract thinking	Blaise Pascal, Albert Einstein, John Dewey, Madame Curie	Working on math or building things during lessons
Visual/Spatial	Reading, maps, charts, drawing, puzzles, visualization	Design, draw, build, create, daydream, look at pictures	Working with pictures and colors, visualizing, drawing	Pablo Picasso, Frank Lloyd Wright, Georgia O'Keefe	Doodling, drawing, daydreaming
Intrapersonal/ Introspective	Understanding self, recognizing strengths and weaknesses, setting goals	Work alone, reflect, pursue interests, set goals	Working alone, self-paced projects, reflecting	Eleanor Roosevelt, Sigmund Freud, Thomas Merton, Buddha	Conflicting with others

(Continued)

Intelligence	Strong In	Likes To	Learns Best	High-End States	Misbehaviors
Interpersonal/ Social	Understanding people, leading, organizing, communicating, resolving conflicts	Have friends, talk to people, join groups, share	Sharing, comparing, relating, interviewing, cooperating	Nelson Mandela, Ronald Reagan, Gandhi, Mother Teresa	Talking, passing notes
Bodily/ Kinesthetic	Athletics, dancing, acting, crafts, using tools, sculpture	Play sports, dance, move around, touch and talk, use body language	Touching, moving, processing knowledge through bodily sensations	Charlie Chaplin, Michael Jordan, Martha Graham, Auguste Rodin	Fidgeting, wandering around the room
Musical/ Rhythmic	Singing, performances remembering melodies, rhythms	Sing, hum, play instrument, listen to music, rap	Rhythm, melody, singing, listening to music and melodies	Stevie Wonder, Leonard Bernstein, Mozart, Ella Fitzgerald	Tapping pencil or feet
Naturalist	Expertise in distinguishing among members of species and charting out these relationships	Categorize and classify things, develop mapping skills, backpacking, hiking, have animals around	Observing, collecting, and comparing things in nature	Charles Darwin, Jane Goodall, E. O. Wilson	Boredom with conventional classroom activities

you, as a parent. Just as students must be taught the alphabet, how to make words, and how to read and write, they must also be taught such things as how to use an active imagination, how to do a graphic presentation, and how to see relationships between different objects in space. Give your children the opportunities and the support needed to exercise and practice using all of their intelligences at home.

As a parent, you know that there's much more to life than school. You know that life success don't always rely on grade point averages. Some children have trouble seeing beyond what happens in school. You can help your young ones gain perspective, and even a little self-esteem boost, by guiding them toward those activities that play to their strengths and offer more opportunities for success.

Don't forget, you know them better than anyone else does. You understand their strengths, weaknesses, and interests more then anyone. Use this information when you help your children choose extracurricular activities. Another consideration that is significant is to sometimes bypass what all the other kids in the neighborhood are doing in favor of something more suited for your kids. You know best!

The next generation offers unlimited possibilities and inconceivable advances. The future not only lies in technology and medical advances, but in your children guided by you and their teachers to help shape their future with satisfaction and confidence. First, you need to believe in yourself and in your children! Then, you must provide them with the love, encouragement, and opportunities that reinforce their self-concept and competence. This is your "gift of love and time" to them for now and in the future.

SOFTWARE THAT ACTIVATES
THE MULTIPLE INTELLIGENCES

Verbal/Linguistic Intelligence
• Word processing programs (Corel WordPerfect)
• Typing tutors (Mavis Beacon Teaches Typing!)
• Desktop publishing programs (Publish It!)
• Electronic references (Encyclopedia Brittanica CD)
• Interactive storybooks (Just Grandma and Me)
• Word games (Missing Links)
• Foreign language instruction and translation software (Easy Translator)
• Website creation software (Front Page)
• Dictation software (Kurzweil Voice Pad)

Logical/Mathematical Intelligence
• Math skills tutorials (Math Blaster)
• Computer programming tutors (LOGO)
• Logic games (King's Rule)
• Science programs (Science Tool Kits)
• Critical thinking programs (Higher Order Thinking Skills [HOTS])
• Database management (Lotus Organizer)
• Financial management software (Quicken Deluxe)
• Science reference guides (Encyclopedia of Science)
• Spreadsheets (Lotus Spreadsheet)

Visual/Spatial Intelligence
• Animation programs (Art and Film Director)
• Draw-and-paint (Dazzle Draw)
• Electronic chess games (Chessmaster)

- Spatial problem-solving games (Tetris)
- Electronic puzzle kits (Living Jigsaws)
- Clip-art programs (The New Print Shop)
- Geometry programs (Sensei's Geometry)
- Graphic presentations of knowledge (World GeoGraph)
- Art history guides (History through Art)
- Home and landscape design software (Complete Land-Designer)
- Maps and atlases (Eyewitness World Atlas)
- Computer-aided design programs (Quick CAD)
- Photo-processing software (Adobe Photo Deluxe)
- Video-processing software (Video Wave)

Bodily/Kinesthetic Intelligence
- Hands-on construction kits that interface with computers (LEGO to LOGO)
- Motion-simulation games (Flight Simulator)
- Virtual reality system software (Dactyl Nightmare)
- Eye-hand coordination games (Shufflepuck Café)
- Tools that plug into computers (Science Toolkit)
- Human anatomy and health reference guides (Body-Works)
- Physical fitness software (Active Trainer)
- Sports software (Golf Pro)

Musical/Rhythmic Intelligence
- Music literature tutors (Exploratorium)
- Singing software [transforms voice input into synthesizer sounds] (Vocalizer)
- Composition software (Music Studio)
- Tone recognition and melody memory enhancers (Arnold)

- Musical instrument digital interfaces, also known as MIDI (Music Quest MIDI Starter System)
- Music instrument instruction software (Interactive Guitar)
- Musical notation programs (Desktop Sheet Music)

Interpersonal/Social Intelligence
- Electronic bulletin boards (Kidsnet)
- Simulation games (Sim City)
- Mailing list programs (My Mail List and Address Book)
- Genealogy programs (Generations)
- Electronic phone books (Streets USA)
- Electronic board games (Chess)

Intrapersonal/Introspective Intelligence
- Personal choice software (Oregon Trail)
- Career counseling software (The Perfect Career)
- Self-understanding software (Emotional IQ Test)
- Fantasy role-play software (Myst)
- Any self-paced program (e.g., many of the preceding programs)

Naturalist Intelligence
- Naturalist reference guides (*National Geographic*)
- Nature simulation programs (Amazon Trail)
- Animal games software (Amazing Animals Activity Center)
- Ecology awareness programs (Magic School Bus Explores the World of Animals)
- Gardening programs (Complete LandDesigner)

Don't Miss the Bus! in learning how your children are special!

Stop! Look! Take Action!

Learn How Your Children Are Special

1. **Emphasize that your children are special in some way.** The question should be: "How are my children smart?" rather than: "How smart are my children?"

2. **Explore the eight types of intelligence:**
   - *Verbal/Linguistic*—ability in reading and writing proficiency
   - *Logical/Mathematical*—ability to reason deductively or inductively
   - *Visual/Spatial*—ability to visualize shapes in three dimensions
   - *Intrapersonal/Introspective*—ability to understand oneself/aware of goals
   - *Interpersonal/Social*—ability to get along with others
   - *Bodily/Kinesthetic*—ability to solve problems/convey ideas with the body

- *Musical/Rhythmic*—ability to be sensitive to rhythm and pitch
- *Naturalist*—ability to distinguish and record information in nature

> *If we succeed in giving the love of learning,*
> *the learning itself is sure to follow.*
>
> —SIR JOHN LUBBOCK

The strategies in this book involve an ongoing process of change for you as well as your children. Your work as a good parent never ends and the rewards of good parenting will have no end either. You will be challenged, over and over again, by your children. In these cases, use the skills you have learned on your journey in *Don't Miss the Bus!* You will be rewarded and continue to have new successes with each stage of growth your children experience. You will enjoy the confidence that you have worked so hard to attain. When you need a little encouragement now and again, refer back to the strategies set out in the journey we just took together so that you *Don't Miss the Bus!* for your destination: your children's school success!

Parents, stress the value of learning to your children, not only in what you say, but in what you do. Express your belief in education as the best means to self-improvement. Seeing and hearing you involved in guiding your young ones in their school success will speak volumes to them. They can hardly miss the message: I am important! My parents care about me! They want the best for me!

As you continue on your journey to help make your children successful students, you will experience the joy and satisfaction that comes from your commitment. In addition to being the most important "constant" in the life of your children, you are loving, knowledgeable, and proactive. You try never to tire in your resolve. As you support the accomplishments of your children, you will come to realize that just your presence, caring, and wisdom make the real difference in your kids' lives. There is no greater joy than to "be there" for your children—no matter what! Your ability to influence your kids' direction rests on your unfailing commitment to the most rewarding job in the world: raising your children to be loving and lovable, caring, and responsible human beings. Yes! You can do it! You have the power within you! Your hard work will pay off. It's up to you now. Good luck to you on your journey to your children's success in school.

A Parent's Prayer

What an awesome job I have
to love, nurture and guide!
Please, Lord, hear my prayer;
throughout the day be at my side.
Let me be the best parent that I can be.
Open their minds and hearts
that they may always see
the best in themselves and others, I pray.
Give me the strength to do
what I should each day.
Keep these precious ones in my charge
always safe from harm and to you, near.
Assist me to teach them right from wrong
without anxiety or fear.
Oh Lord, guide me now to give them
the benefit of the best start.
Help them grow healthy and happy.
Then, I'll know I've done my part.

MARY ANN SMIALEK

The Journey into Cyberspace

Internet Safety

○ What should I know about the Internet to help my children?

○ How can I ensure my children's safety on the World Wide Web?

○ How can I guide my children to be cyberspace smart?

7

THE WORLD WIDE WEB connects millions of people around the globe with an instant means of communication and is a powerful tool for information gathering. It is important for you, as a parent, to educate yourself about technology and the opportunities for learning and fun it offers your children. "Cyberspace," the "World Wide Web," the "Information Superhighway," and the "Internet" are all words used to describe the most innovative and exciting learning tool of the twenty-first century.

At the touch of your keyboard you can "visit" Australia, view a copy of the Declaration of Independence, and watch a tsunami or a tornado come to life on your computer screen. You can instantly send "mail" to a relative or friend in another city, state, or country. The alternatives for knowledge and communication are endless. The sheer volume of things to do online—places to go, news to hear, and stories with illustrations to see and read—can be overwhelming! It can also sometimes make it difficult to find the exact information that you want.

Most people who use online services have positive experiences, but like any endeavor—cooking, traveling, or attending school—there are some risks. The online world, like the rest of society, is made up of a wide array of people. Most are decent, law-abiding, and respectful, but some may be rude, obnoxious, insulting, or even exploitative. Like radio, movies, and television before the Internet, there is much concern about children's use of this new medium. Learning yourself and teaching your children to make wise choices is one of the most important things you can do. Your children benefit from being online, but they can also be targets of crime and exploitation in this as in any other environment. Trusting, curious, and anxious to explore this new world of the Internet, your children need your supervision and common-sense advice. Help them make sure that their experiences in cyberspace are healthy, happy, and productive.

Remember, it is not the technology but how you and your children use it that makes the difference.

WHAT YOU SHOULD KNOW
ABOUT THE INTERNET

Help your children learn how to be "cyberspace smart" in order to better safeguard themselves in various situations. It's vital for you, as a parent, to first educate yourself and then your children about new technology opportunities for learning and fun. Just as there are many radio stations, television channels, movies, and videos, there are many places to visit on the Web. Here are some definitions to help you get more acquainted to the possibilities the Internet offers:

> **"Websites"** are places that are informative and are sponsored by many different organizations—educational, nonprofit, or companies—that want to market their products and services. In addition to these sites, thousands of other sites are created by individuals and groups that have a positive mission or hidden agenda. Their ideas, concerns, or warnings are expressed in depth on their sites.
>
> **"E-mail"** (electronic mail) makes it possible for you to send a written message to one person or a group of hundreds in your hometown, state, country, or worldwide in seconds.
>
> **"Chat rooms"** are Information Superhighway sites that target particular subject areas like BMX racing, video games, politics, and so on. Interested users of these sites can converse with others by typing questions and receiving typed answers in response.
>
> **"Usenet group sites"** are electronic bulletin boards with postings on specific subjects. Most Usenet news groups are unregulated.

It is in your children's best interests to guide them in their selections that will be helpful with their homework and special interests. Spending time online with your children is one of the best ways to learn and to teach responsibility, proper conduct, and values that are important to you and your youngsters' future. They need guidance in finding websites that are helpful and not harmful to them. It is also significant to teach your young ones "netiquette"— that is, how to fittingly conduct themselves online. It is proper to use regular type—no bold, underline, italics, or all caps (all of these typefaces indicate strong emotions such as yelling, anger, or frustration). It is also good manners for your children to wait, read, and learn in chat rooms until they get a sense of what others are talking about.

If you don't have access to a computer at home, your children's school library, public library, or local college library have computers for public use. Many of these organizations also provide recommended websites that offer classes for adults as well as for student users.

Check with your children's school. Special programs or workshops may be offered for you to learn about the Internet and how you can guide your young ones to safe websites. You should always examine websites that your youngsters frequent for gender, racial, or other biases that you know are inappropriate for your young ones.

INFORMATION TO PROTECT YOUR CHILDREN

The best way to ensure your children's safety on the Internet is to supervise them at home and at the library. It is impossible to always be with them, so you have to remind them to make informed choices. Just as you teach your young ones rules about strangers and new situations, you must provide some rules for online communication. Get to know the services your children use. Offer your children these Internet safety tips:

1. Never give out any personal information: name, address, phone number, or online password
2. If you see something on the Internet that you don't understand or that scares you, tell your parent or teacher immediately
3. Don't respond to messages that make you feel uncomfortable or confused
4. Never, never agree to meet a person that you've met online unless your parents know about it and approve
5. Remember that everything you hear and see online may not be true

Set reasonable rules and guidelines for your children's computer use. Discuss these rules and post them near the computer as a reminder. Try to make computer use a family activity. Consider keeping the computer in a family room rather than in your children's bedroom. Get to know their online friends just as you get to know all of their other friends.

The majority of websites are safe, but you need to concern yourself with the sites that contain violence, sex, and other subject matters that are not appropriate for your children. It's important to establish clear guidelines for your youngsters' Internet use. Software packages that block certain types of websites are not always effective. Your parental guidance is the best defense to keep inappropriate or offensive and harmful sites from your children.

KEY INTERNET SAFETY POINTS TO REMEMBER

- First, understand technology
- Watch your children while they are online
- Listen and talk to your young ones when they are offline
- Know how to check where they have been online
- Sometimes you have to say "no"
- Create a set of rules with your children
- Place the written rules in a place where they can be seen and referred to often

A NOTE ABOUT BUYING COMPUTERS AND SOFTWARE

Several reputable nonprofit organizations review software and CD-ROM programs. You can sample a program at your children's school or at your local library. Call ahead to see if these organizations can support you in selecting the right software for your children and your particular computer. Remember, do your homework before you buy a certain computer and make sure the software programs you choose are compatible with the computer you choose. If you are thinking about buying a computer or upgrading an old one, first consider the ages of your children and their current and future computer needs. Consider waiting until they are a little older when perhaps they'll be able to appreciate a faster modem or higher resolution images. By that time, prices will surely come down and computer technology will be improved.

Filtering software products can be installed on your computer to limit and monitor Internet use. Such products can block access to objectionable sites. In addition, they will log where the computer user has visited, often in a way that is more "user friendly" than getting the same information from a Web browser. Filtering software is not a perfect solution, however. It often inadvertently blocks access to positive sites. "Filters" often need to be updated, creating a time lag in which newer inappropriate sites are not screened. Filtering software can be beneficial but you must understand both its uses and limitations. Even the best filtering software is no substitute for parental involvement in your children's Internet use.

Web browser software programs leave "trails" that can be examined to determine which websites the user has visited. America Online and Microsoft Network offer parental controls. These controls allow you to designate different levels of access for each of your children. You can configure them to block Instant Messages, chat rooms, private chats, or the possibility of downloading files. In addition, you may restrict your youngsters' e-mail or block files attached to e-mails. A "buddy list" feature may be used to set up a safe list of friends. Inappropriate websites can also be reported via these controls.

You will make a difference in your children's journey to cyberspace by being knowledgeable and proactive about the Internet so that your young ones will enjoy the benefits of being Web-wise.

Visit the American Library Association's website www.ala.org/parentspage/greatsites/ for "50+ Great Web Sites" and the "Parent's Guide to the Information Superhighway." For rules and tools for families online, see www.cybersmartkids.com.au/.

A CHILD'S PLEDGE TO ONLINE SAFETY

I promise to talk to my parents so that we can set up rules for going online. We will decide together on the time of day, the length of time to be online, and the appropriate sites for me to visit. I will not break these rules without my parent's permission.

Stop! Look! Take Action!

Know and Follow Internet Safety Information to Protect Your Children

1. Internet safety tips:
- Never give out any personal information: name, address, phone number, or online password

- If you see something on the Internet that you don't understand or that scares you, tell your parents or teacher immediately
- Don't respond to messages that make you feel uncomfortable or confused
- Never, never agree to meet a person that you've met online unless your parents know about it and approve
- Remember that everything you hear and see online may not be true

2. Key internet safety points to remember:
- First, understand technology
- Watch your children while they are online
- Listen and talk to your young ones when they are offline
- Know how to check where they have been online
- Sometimes you have to say "no"
- Create a set of rules with your children
- Place written rules in a place where they can be seen and referred to often

The Parent Who Gets Ahead Is The One Who Does More Than Is Necessary and Keeps On Doing It!

Strategy Intervention Form

Take a minute to reflect on your observations of a positive strategy that you put into action. What worked? What didn't work? Mark the areas that apply with A+ for a positive experience and A– for ones that you need to work on another time. Reflecting on a situation after using positive strategy intervention is helpful when focusing on the things that will work with your particular child. Remember, these skill-building strategies do not uniformly fit every child in every situation. My best advice to you is to reflect, monitor, and adjust!

Name of strategy: _____

Date: _____

Consider your child's reactions with you. _____

_____

Weigh your child's interactions with other children.

_____

_____

Relate how you encouraged your child to expect a "great deal" of him- or herself.

_____

_____

Convey values (e.g., respect for authority and other's property) you stressed.

_____

_____

Relate "good" examples that you shared with your child. (Actions speak louder than words.) _____

_____

_____

Express how you supplied a strong support system to your child. _____

_____

Consider your responsibilities and your child's in the future.

_____

Share special encouragement to make the "next time" more positive. _____

_____

Key lesson learned from this strategy:

_____

_____

RECOMMENDED BOOKS

Armstrong, Thomas. 2000. *Multiple Intelligences in the Classroom.* Alexandria, Va.: Association for Supervision and Curriculum Development.

Brooks, Robert, and Goldstein, Sam. 2001. *Raising Resilient Children.* Chicago: Contemporary.

———. 2002. *Nurturing Resilience in Our Children: Answers to the Most Important Parenting Questionnaires.* Chicago: Contemporary.

Brooks, Whitney, and McGuinness, Tracy. 2000. *School Smarts: All the Right Answers to Homework, Teachers, Popularity and More!* Middleton, Wisc.: Pleasant Company Publications.

Clark, Rosemarie, et al. 1999. *The School-Savvy Parent: 365 Insider Tips to Help You Help Your Child.* Minneapolis, Minn.: Free Spirit.

Davidson, Alan, and Davidson, Robert. 1996. *How Good Parents Raise Great Kids.* New York: Warner.

Diamond, Marion, and Hopson, Janet. 1999. *Magic Trees of the Mind: How to Nurture Your Child's Intelligence, Creativity and Healthy Emotions.* New York: Penguin.

Dinkmeyer, Don Sr., McKay, Gary, and Dinkmeyer, Don Jr. 1997. *Systematic Training for Effective Parenting (STEP): The Parent's Handbook.* Circle Pines, Minn.: American Guidance Service.

Goldstein, Sam, Hagar, Kristy, and Brooks, Robert. 2002. *Seven Steps to Help Your Children Worry Less: A Family Guide.* Plantation, Fla.: Specialty.

Heininger, J. E., and Weiss, S. K. 2001. *From Chaos to Calm: Effective Parenting of Challenging Children with ADHD and Other Behavioral Problems.* New York: Pedigree.

Ingersoll, B. D., and Goldstein, Sam. 2001. *Lonely, Sad, and Angry: How to Help Your Unhappy Child.* Plantation, Fla.: Specialty.

Karres Shearin, Erika. 2002. *Make Your Kids Smarter, 50 Top Teacher Tips for Grades K–8.* Kansas City, Miss.: Andrews McMeel.

Peters, Ruth. 2000. *Overcoming Underachieving: A Simple Plan to Boost Your Kids' Grades and End the Homework Hassles.* New York: Broadway.

Schank, Roger. 2000. *Coloring Outside the Lines: Raising a Smarter Kid by Breaking All the Rules.* New York: HarperCollins.

Smialek, Mary Ann. 2001. Team Strategies for Success: Doing What Counts in Education. Lanham, Md.: Scarecrow Press.

Stipek, Deborah, and Seal, Kathy. 2001. *Motivated Minds: Raising Children to Love Learning.* New York: Owl.

Willis, Mariaemma, and Kindle-Hodson, Victoria. 1999. *Discover Your Child's Learning Style: Children Learn in Unique Ways—Here's the Key to Every Child's Learning Success.* Roseville, Calif.: Prima.

Wolf, Jill. 1992. *Teachers Are . . .* Yellow Springs, Ohio: Antioch.

Zentall, Sydney, and Goldstein, Sam. 1999. *Seven Steps to Homework Success: A Family Guide for Solving Common Homework Problems.* Plantation, Fla.: Specialty.

RECOMMENDED WEBSITES

Please note that these websites were current at the time of publication. Please be advised that they may not be available at some point in the future. If a site is unavailable to you and you need particular information, you may contact me at www.schoolsuccess.info.

www.familyeducation.com
Many links for parents with grade-specific advice for school success.

www.childrenspartnership.org/prnt/prnt.html
Offers online resources for good parenting.

www.eduhound.com
Provides many links to various education-related sites.

www.kidport.com
A children's site to help youngsters excel in school.

www.scholastic.com
Gives many ideas for learning/enrichment activities for students.

www.par-inst.com/resources/default.htm
Suggestions for parent involvement sponsored by
The Parent's Institute.

www.websmart kids.org
Guides children in Internet use.

www.superkids.com
Online reviews of educational software programs.

www.syvum.com
Site provides online software that you can download.

www.ldonline.com
Offers many resources and advice for parenting children with learning disabilities.

www.schwablearning.org
Developed especially for parents of children who
have learning problems.

www.readingrockets.org
Provides news, practical information, expert advice,
and resources for parents and teachers.

www.startribune.com/homework_help
Offers homework help.

**http: school.discovery.com/homeworkhelp/
bjpinchbeck**
Offers homework help.

www.geocities.com/Athens/Ithaca/4845/mitheory.html
Website devoted entirely to collected material regard-

ing the discovery of multiple intelligences by psychologist Howard Gardener.

www.allianceforchildhood.org
This site is committed to fostering and respecting each child's inherent right to a healthy, developmentally appropriate childhood.

www.connectforkids.org
Online action and information center for adults who care about kids. There are articles affecting children with state-by-state links. Site offers two free e-newsletters.

www.lionlamb.org
Website publishes an annual "Dirty Dozen" list of toys it considers highly objectionable, along with a companion list of more appropriate toys.

www.playingforkeeps.org
It offers a look at the research on the benefits of play. It also offers ideas on play activities for parents.

www.familylife1st.org
This site is concerned about families and their overscheduled lives.

www.hyperparenting.com
Offers parents a dozen practical tips for countering efforts to overschedule children.

www.familynightamonth.com
This website highlights the importance of families spending time together.

www.truceteachers.com
Site shares a concern with parents who have a concern about how their children's entertainment and toys affect learning and behavior.

www.tvp.org
Devoted to helping parents understand the effect of television viewing on their families. It also offers suggestions for alternatives to television viewing.

www.firmonline.org
Site provides a forum for parents who want to share their lessons and concerns and receive practical tools and information.

www.samgoldstein.com
This strong site focuses on changing the lives of challenged children. Sam Goldstein is known for his ability to summarize and present to parents current research in practical ways.

www.drrobertbrooks.com
Robert Brooks' informative site focuses on resilience, self-esteem, motivation, and family relationships for parents of special needs children.

www.raisingresilientkids.com
Site disseminates information to assist adults to raise, support, and develop stress-hardy children.

PARENT SUPPORT SYSTEMS AND ORGANIZATIONS

Coalition for Community Schools
www.communityschools.org/strategies
www.ccs@iel.org
1001 Connecticut Avenue NW, Suite 310
Washington, DC 20036
Phone: (202) 822-8405
Fax: (202) 872-4050

The Coalition for Community Schools is the national organization improving student learning and strengthening schools, families, and communities.

Federation for Community Planning
www.wleatherberry@fcp.org
www.fcp.org
1226 Huron Road, Suite 300
Cleveland, OH 44115-1702
Phone: (216) 781-2944
Fax: (216) 781-2988

The Federation for Community Planning provides strategic leadership on targeted issues in the field of health and human services for the community to ensure comprehensive and effective plans and action.

Learning First Alliance

www.learningfirst.org
1001 Connecticut Avenue NW, Suite 335
Washington, DC 20036
Phone: (202) 296-5220
Fax: (202) 296-3256

The Learning First Alliance is a permanent partnership of twelve leading educational associations that have come together to improve student learning in America's public elementary and secondary schools.

MegaSkills Education Center

www.megaskillshsi.org/Default.htm
The Home and School Institute
1500 Massachusetts Avenue NW
Washington, DC 20005

The MegaSkills Education Center is devoted to academic development and character education.

National Coalition for Parent Involvement in Education (NCPIE)

www.ncpie.org
3929 Old Lee Highway, Suite 91-A
Fairfax, VA 22030-2401
Phone: (703) 359-8973
Fax: (703) 359-0972

The NCPIE's mission is to advocate the involvement of parents and families in education and to foster relationships between the home, school, and community to enhance education.

Parent-Teacher Association (PTA)

www.pta.org
National PTA Headquarters
330 North Wabash Avenue, Suite 2100
Chicago, IL 60611
Phone: (800) 307-4782
Fax: (321) 670-6783

The National PTA is the largest volunteer child-advocacy organization in the United States. A nonprofit association of parents, educators, students, and other citizens active in their schools and communities, the PTA is a leader in reminding our nation of its obligations to children.

PTO Today Online (Parent-Teacher Organization)

www.ptotoday.com/index.html
PTO Today
Circulation
2 Celinda Drive
Franklin, MA 02038

Founded in the spring of 1999, PTO Today has quickly established itself in the center of the parent group world as a valuable resource for parents.

Partnership for Family Involvement in Education (PFIE)
www.pfie.ed.gov
U.S. Department of Education
400 Maryland Avenue SW
Washington, DC 20202-8173
E-mail: partner@ed.gov

The PFIE gives its mission as "to increase opportunities for families to be more involved in their children's learning at school and at home and to use family-school-community partnerships to strengthen schools and improve student achievement."

Project Parents, Inc.
www.projectparents.org
46 Beach Street, Suite 502
Boston, MA 02111
Phone: (617) 451-0360

Project Parents offers workshops on several topics, including helping children become better readers.

ABOUT THE AUTHOR

MARY ANN SMIALEK, ED.D., director of Quest Solutions, is an experienced educator in both regular and special education, specializing in the remediation of specific learning problems. She is a leading speaker and author on home-school partnerships and on motivation and team strategies. Dr. Smialek is the editor of the American Society for Quality Education Division's *QED News* and chair of the Quality in Education Focus Group. Contact her at smialek@mail.com or visit her Website: maryannsmialek.com.